**The Night Sun:**
**Our Wounds, Prometheus In Evin, Poems**
and
**Leave To Remain**

**Our Wounds**, Jannatie Ataie's first play written in English, was taken on tour by Intercut, The International Cultural Unity Theatre. Jannatie Ataie's own company, The Mazdak Theatre Group, founded in 1982 to preserve Iranian theatrical culture, first performed **Prometheus In Evin** at The Royal Court Theatre in 1987. The following year a new version, translated into English by Jannatie Ataie, opened at the Young Vic Theatre, London.

Jannatie Ataie 'provides a brilliant and compelling universal story of men demeaning themselves in the service of tyranny which must place him in the forefront of international playwrights today.'                     Victoria Brittain, *Guardian*

'A gripping and moving story.'          Alex Renton, *Independent*

'In this powerful play of opposition . . . the characterisation is chillingly and unsentimentally real and the language swings eloquently from the sharp, rhythmic soliloquies of suffering to the lyricism of emotion recollected in tranquillity.'
                          Claire Armitstead, *Financial Times*

The selection of poems included here were written over a period of twenty-five years; some of them have entered into Iranian culture as popular songs. **Leave To Remain**, a screenplay commissioned by Channel 4 and directed by Les Blair, was co-written by Rob Ritchie who has also written an introduction to this volume.

**Iraj Jannatie Ataie** was born in Mashad 'North East Iran' in 1947 and educated at Tehran's School For Dramatic Arts. He was arrested by the Shah for writing plays and poems and escaped to England ten years ago, where he has been living ever since. His play **A Cry With Sewn Lips** was staged at The Royal Court Theatre in 1985 and **I Miss My War** was premièred at the Almeida Theatre in November 1989.

**Methuen New Theatrescripts** series offers frontline intelligence
of the most original and exciting work from the fringe.

# The Night Sun

## Our Wounds
## Prometheus In Evin
## Poems
*Iraj Jannatie Ataie*

## Leave To Remain
*Rob Ritchie and Iraj Jannatie Ataie*

**Methuen Drama**

**A Methuen New Theatrescript**

*This collection first published in Great Britain as a paperback original
in 1989 by Methuen Drama, Michelin House, 81 Fulham Road,
London SW3 6RB and distributed in the United States of America by
HEB Inc., 70 Court Street, Portsmouth, New Hampshire 03801.*

*A CIP Catalogue Record for this book is available from the British
Library*

ISBN 0-413-62250-9

Typeset by **$\nearrow$** Tek Art Ltd, Croydon
Printed in Great Britain by Cox and Wyman Ltd, Reading

This book is dedicated to the memory of my parents, who died without being permitted to see their three sons exiled for more than ten years.

## Acknowledgements

I would like to thank the following people:

Mary and Nasser Memarzia
Faramarz Aslani
Neil Johnston
Richard McKane
Les Blair
Linda Brandon
Stella Shmidt
Touraj and Nader Jannatie Ataie
Phil Young

# Introduction

A few years ago, I travelled with Iraj Jannatie Ataie – a selection of whose plays and poems is published here in English for the first time – to Düsseldorf in West Germany. It was a miserable, depressing journey. Neither of us had much money, though we did have prospects. Immediately before leaving London we had sat in the back of a car outside Victoria station and signed the contract commissioning **Leave To Remain**, our first joint venture as screenwriters. Recruitment into the British film industry didn't take long – there was a brief discussion about what in perpetuity meant – but we quickly discovered the cheque that would have allowed us to travel in style and comfort would take a little longer. So, several pounds short of an air fare, we had to make do with the overnight ferry to Ostend and a slow haul on an unlit train across Belgium. Somewhere along the way, long after we'd run out of cigarettes and the train had run out of drinking water, Iraj peered at me through the darkness and said, 'Now you know what it's like being a poor, bloody foreigner'. As an exiled writer, arguably Iran's finest living poet and dramatist, Iraj has an acute eye for the absurdity of life and he was greatly amused at the miseries of our journey. No sooner had we left London it seemed than things began to go wrong. We mistakenly took someone else's seats on the train to Dover and were moved the moment we settled. On the ferry, what was probably the only passenger afflicted with seasickness that night took the trouble of staggering out of his way to throw up at our feet. Iraj, courteous to a fault, thanked him and suggested I ask directions to the cafeteria. Then, as if to confirm our banishment from the real world, the duty free shop, site of much needed cheap refreshment, closed for business minutes before we discovered where it was. All night we were moved on, turned away or woken up to be questioned. To make matters worse, when we eventually got to Düsseldorf, we failed to achieve what we had come to do.

Our destination was the British Consulate, an ugly, fortified building in the suburbs of the city; our purpose, to persuade the authorities to issue an Iranian woman who had come from Tehran with a visa enabling her to visit London with her little daughter. The trip was to be no holiday. The girl needed a minor operation to mend a cleft palate and the continuing ravages of the Gulf war meant there was no prospect of her having it performed in Iran. All available surgeons were busily patching up Khomeini's battered soldiers. Iraj and I had found a private doctor prepared to do the operation in London, assembled the money to pay for it and now came to escort mother and child to England. If we had had a rough ride, it was nothing to the journey undertaken by the woman. As the British embassy in Tehran was closed, her only means of getting to Europe was a ten-day tourist visa to Germany. This had taken months to arrange. Accompanied by her sister and brother-in-law, she had flown to Cologne with her daughter and laboured across an unfamiliar country to rendezvous with us in Düsseldorf. When we all met up outside the station, the little girl danced and clapped as she spotted Iraj, seemingly unaffected by her journey. There was a simple reason for this. Iraj was her uncle, known to her from a photograph, and the women were his two sisters. They hadn't seen each other for six years, ever since Iraj had escaped to London to avoid further imprisonment for writing plays and poems. Like most people, I've witnessed many a reunion in my time, seen the first tumble of questions lapse into awkward silence as the strangeness of separation takes hold. But I've never felt the pain of exile quite so keenly as I felt it that afternoon. Iraj had changed. His sisters had changed. And there was nowhere to sit and talk about it.

Within a matter of days, Iraj and I were back in London and his sisters were on a plane to Tehran. There had been few successes at the visa desk on the morning we called at the consulate. A delegation of Chinese businessmen got clearance once an interpreter had been found. But an Englishman anxious to get his Czech fiancée to Knutsford in time for their wedding was refused. The girl had once been deported for working illegally which meant the case had to be referred to London. 'But we've already arranged the wedding', the man said, nudging his fiancée forward as if sight of her would somehow melt the heart of the immigration officer as it so obviously had his own. The woman behind the desk was unmoved. 'You'll just have to cancel it.' Watching this exchange, I realised that as far as the officials were concerned, everyone standing in line was an undesirable alien until they proved otherwise. I've no idea what distant turmoil had brought so many anxious faces to plead for a passage to

# Introduction

England. I was there because a little girl needed her mouth fixed. But, as I soon found out, no one was more undesirable to the British state that day than an Iranian. Foolishly, I'd imagined my status as a British citizen would somehow help matters. I had a sheaf of documents proving the facts of our case, x-rays of the girl's face, the phone number of an eminent plastic surgeon and, more to the point, I could argue in English. Before I could do anything, however, I was told no Iranians could be issued with visas without a full interview. This seemed reasonable enough until I discovered the catch. The first available appointment was three months away. If Iraj's sister wanted to bring her daughter to London she would have to go back to Tehran and return to Düsseldorf at four-thirty on a Thursday afternoon the following October. Even if this had been a practical proposal – it seemed unlikely the Germans would let her visit a second time – there was of course no guarantee the interview would be successful. It would have been kinder and more honest to say no.

Every refugee has a story to tell of the family and friends they left behind. And every refugee knows how hard it is to gain admission to what we like to think of as the free world. The writer of the present volume has had more than his fair share of personal suffering and one day I hope he will tell his own story. For the moment, Iraj has other priorities. As a poet, it has been his task to give voice to the struggles of his people, to keep alive a literary and theatrical tradition that has been savagely destroyed by Khomeini and his followers. He has carried out this responsibility with immense courage and determination, refusing to be silenced despite the ever present threats against his life. Salman Rushdie was not the first writer to incur the displeasure of the Ayatollah. The name of Iraj Jannatie Ataie has long been on the list; his crime to speak of freedom, peace and plenty in such a way that those who hear his words do not forget them. Others will have to assess the literary achievement. Here, I can only salute a comrade and friend and urge English readers to listen to what he has to say.

Rob Ritchie
August 1989

# Our Wounds

*For Danny Boyle*

**Our Wounds** was first staged by Intercut at Battersea Arts Centre and toured London and the Edinburgh Festival in 1981 with the following cast:

| | |
|---|---|
| **Kaveh The Blacksmith** | William Jorite |
| | Deborah Levy |
| | Mark Pawelek |
| | Cathy McDonough |
| | Libby Wilson |
| **Zahhak** | Wayne Nicol |
| **The Devil** | Mozaffar Shafeie |

Other characters are played by members of the cast.

*Directed and designed by* Iraj Jannatie Ataie

# Act One

Scene One

*The stage is bare.* **Zahhak** *is galloping around the stage, hunting.*

**Narrator** Ladies and gentlemen, our play is based on a myth, a myth from ancient Iran, the myth of Kaveh and Zahhak: Zahhak the prince, Kaveh the blacksmith. According to this myth, one day the devil appears to Zahhak as a visitor, and tempts him to become a king.

**Zahhak** *is galloping and hunting. Suddenly he sees the devil.*

**Zahhak** Who are you?

**Devil** A merchant. Who are you?

**Zahhak** Zahhak.

**Devil** The king?

**Zahhak** No, just Zahhak.

**Devil** Do you want to be a king? With swift-footed horses? Beautiful women? Wealth? Armies? Palaces? Hunting grounds?

**Zahhak** I love hunting.

**Devil** Then you want to be a king.

**Zahhak** What must I do?

**Devil** I've been sent to make you a king, if you wish.

**Zahhak** How?

**Devil** Simple . . . just obey me.

**Zahhak** Kings don't obey anyone.

**Devil** You're not a king yet.

**Zahhak** (*pause*) Just . . . obey you? (*Pause.*) All right.

**Devil** Do you swear to obey me?

**Zahhak** I swear.

**Zahhak** *gets off his horse, sends it away and kneels before the devil. The* **Devil** *crowns* **Zahhak**.

**Narrator**  So Zahhak pledges with the devil and becomes a king. But the devil has an unfinished job to do . . . kissing the king's shoulders.

**Devil**  (*kisses* **Zahhak**'s *shoulders*)  Now you are a king.

**Narrator**  And there was a mystery in the devil's kisses: the evil seeds of dragons. And then grew snakes . . . the royal flags. . . on the royal shoulders.

Scene Two

*A public place. The* **Herald** *blows a trumpet, calling the people together. The people gather round the* **Herald**.

**Herald**  People of the town! Know and be aware that Prince Zahhak has defeated and killed the tyrant king in a national war against the enemies of the country. This war between Prince Zahhak and his father took ninety long seconds in which the prince, with exceptional bravery, succeeded in stabbing his father in the back when the king set foot in the court hall. Your hero covered the battlefield with the dirty blood of his father, and ended the war to your advantage. People, know and be aware that Zahhak is not only a wise, kind and just king, but also the messenger of God, and is gifted with the miracle of snakes on his shoulders; snakes which feed on the brains of the people's enemies who oppose the king's rule.

To show your appreciation for such a king, it is decreed that your direct and indirect taxes shall be doubled and paid before the appointed time. We have confidence that obeying the new law will help you in both worlds. May God be always with you.
   The King's Advisor,
   The Prime Minister,
   The Minister of Finance,
   Lord Merchant. (*He bows.*)

**Young Man**  Snakes . . . kings . . . messengers . . . congratulations. All that's missing are the dead.

*The people laugh.*

Scene Three

*A bazaar. A* **Man** *and a* **Young Man** *are working downstage. Two soldiers walk around among the people looking for the* **Young Man**, *and reach the men working.*

**First Soldier**  We have orders from the king to arrest you.

**Young Man**  Why?

**First Soldier**  For being an enemy of the people.

**Man**  An enemy of the people? But he is from the people . . . with the people. All the people know this . . .

**Second Soldier**  He has opposed the king.

**First Soldier**  And this means being an enemy of the people.

**Second Soldier**  And this will be the fate of any objector, who doesn't obey the orders of the king.

*They take the* **Young Man** *away.*

Scene Four

*A prison: the soldiers are whipping the* **Young Man**.

**Young Man**  And these are the four seasons of our year, from year to year . . . being arrested . . . being imprisoned . . . being tortured . . . and being executed; and the fear of death is ruling us, the people. Every suspicious look . . . every unfamiliar smell . . . and every strange face, in our time, is the presence of death embodied by the secret informers, spying among us. The days of nightmares.

Every footstep . . . every tap . . . every unexpected sound, in our nights, is the sound of death, which has worn the uniform of the ruler's guards, storming our houses. The nights of fear.

Scene Five

*A bazaar.*

**First Woman**  If we could migrate to another land.

**First Man**  Where?

**First Woman**  Anywhere but here.

**First Man**  For us, anywhere is here . . . poverty and work and poverty.

**First Woman**  Animals live better than we do.

**First Man**  More free . . .

**First Woman**  Less frightened . . .

**First Man**  More independent.

*Pause.*

**Second Woman**  The years of fear . . . the years of misery.

**Second Man**  It won't stay like this.

**Second Woman**  What if it does?

**Second Man**  The earth will explode.

**Second Woman**  Someone must do something.

**Second Man**  Who?

*Pause.*

**Third Man**  From sunrise to sundown, we claw the bare soil, under the hot sun on the heated ground. And when the year is over, when it is the harvest time . . . our share is a sack of wheat and our blood-stained sickle and plough. Stained by the blood of our youth and labour and . . .

**Third Woman**  We have hope yet . . .

**Third Man**  And the blood of our hope.

**Third Woman**  I have saved my last bangle, the first memorial of your mother . . .

*Pause.*

**Fourth Woman**  There aren't many men left.

**Fourth Man**  From pasture to pasture, the land is barren of our women.

**Fourth Woman**  From step to step, they are our youngsters sleeping under the ground.

**Fourth Man**   The houses are empty.

**Fourth Man**   And the prisons are full.


Scene Six

*A bazaar.*

**A Woman**   It seems like yesterday. It was sundown when he
came in . . . as always . . . every night . . . tired, hungry and sad.
He took a glance at the baby, a glance at me. While having
dinner I asked him, 'What will happen?' He shrugged his
shoulders. I said, 'How long?' He said, 'When the child is a
year old, our savings will be enough to do something.' He put
his hand in his pocket and gave me his day's wages to put
aside. He had been doing that every night for the past two
years, saying, 'One day we must buy a piece of land, a piece of
land good enough to work on. To work on for ourselves. A
piece of land for our today and our children's tomorrow.'

Two full years, from sunrise to sundown, he sweated his guts
out on the master's land. Winters he crossed the path to find a
job in the cities. When the child cried, he smiled, he smiled and
he listened.

His eyes were shining. He put his hand, his wounded, rough
and heavy hand, on my belly. It was hot. Too hot. Then my
body turned hot. He said, 'I want more, more. Our land will
feed us, all of us.' In the middle of the night, when we were
asleep, wet, satisfied, satisfied and tired, there was a knock at
the door. There was a *heavy* knock at the door. Before I could
reach the door, before we could reach the door, they had
broken it down and made their way in. All drunk. The
drunken sons of the master. Did they want food? Did they
want wine? Did they want somewhere to sleep? They wanted
women. They were yelling and screaming. He fell to their
feet . . . we fell to their feet. One of them put his hand to my
chest . . . tore my dress to . . . to . . . He ran to the safe box,
opened its doors and poured all the money at their feet.
Choked with anger, he said, 'Take it, all of it . . . leave my wife
alone.' The master's sons, when they saw the money, stopped,
quietly looked at each other, took the money and went.

Next morning, when he was leaving, the child was crying. I was crying. He . . . he was smiling and crying. He took his axe, he took his sickle and he went, went. Since he has gone, people say the two sons of the master have disappeared. It seems like yesterday.

Scene Seven

*Execution yard: the* **King** *and the* **Devil** *are there. The two soldiers escort the* **Young Man** *upstage and stop, leaving him. They march downstage, turn and execute him.*

**Devil**  We killed him. We had to. Why?

*The* **King** *and the* **Devil** *laugh.*

Because we have to feed the snakes so that they can stay alive. The snakes must stay alive so that the king can stay alive. The king must stay alive so that the country can stay alive. The country must stay alive so that the people can stay alive. The people must stay alive so we can kill them and feed the snakes.

*The* **King** *and the* **Devil** *laugh.*

**Narrator**  And the dragon king, who had become a king by killing his father, ruled over the people's lives and belongings, under the teachings of the devil in the clothes of the merchant, who as he gathered more wealth, bellowed the fire of the king's lust for blood and soil.

Scene Eight

*The victorious* **Zahhak** *and the* **Devil** *enter the palace,* **Zahhak** *on the shoulders of the people, who are blindfolded.*

**Devil**  Checkmate. Rulership is like playing chess. You . . . as a king . . . have your pawns, and your close servants. Your enemy has the same power. If he kills your people . . . sorry, your pawns . . . it doesn't matter . . . you can kill his people too. Take care of your bishops, knights, queen, etc. But whenever you think it is necessary to sacrifice, to dedicate, don't hesitate . . . don't wait. Send your knights . . . your bishops . . . and even your queen to your enemy, and remain in charge . . . and rule secure.

**Zahhak** If I lose my people . . . sorry, my pawns . . . and my close servants . . . then the enemy can kill me easily . . .

**Devil** Wrong. Kings will remain on the chess board, even if defeated.

**Zahhak** Safe enough!

**Devil** After all this, there will be a question: 'Would you like another game?'

**Zahhak** And in the next game I will still be king.

**Devil** And it will always be the same for your close servants and the people . . . I mean the pawns . . .

## Scene Nine

**Narrator** So Zahhak, the dragon king, started to gather armies, plan war games, launch military attacks and conquer the world.

*A battlefield. The people and the soldiers march and storm each other, and kill the enemy.*

**Narrator** First country. Resistance: three months. The number of people killed: 120,000. The defeated king, the ministers, the merchants and their families, after paying tribute, were condemned to continue to rule.

*A shelter. The peasants are asleep. The soldiers break the door in and rape them, kill them and go.*

**Narrator** Fourth country. Resistance: four weeks. The number of people killed: 70,000. The defeated king, the ministers and merchants were reinstated as the fathers-in-law of the victorious king.

## Scene Ten

*A public house.*

**A Woman** It was about noon that the savage yells and sound of horses' hooves filled the village air. We ran to an empty underground reservoir, we women, children and old men. Young men stood to defend with sickles, spades and picks. The soldiers burnt all houses, massacred all men. They didn't even have mercy on cats and dogs.

We were dying of fear in that empty shelter. The endless nights passed. The soldiers that had stayed on and made camp were roasting our cows and our sheep. They ate and grew obese, while we were dying of hunger under there.

An old man among us, who from hunger and horror lost his mind, pushed away his sick wife and ran towards the manhole yelling. Before he could reach the ladder they got him, knocked him down and covered his mouth with their hands, hard. Like a raging bull that is about to be branded, he writhed wildly and struggled. They beat him . . . they beat him. His sick wife said, 'If the soldiers know we are here they will cut us to pieces . . . beat him, make him quiet.'

And those of us who hadn't lost our minds from fear, started to make him quiet. The groans of the hungry, the groans of us all, echoed in that empty shelter.

All of us from hunger had eaten the dry bushes in the shelter. We had eaten everything, even the milk of a woman who had left her newborn child outside. That woman, who had become our mother many times, was groaning, milkless and breathless. The old man's look had quietened down, so we left him. He yelled again; his sick wife crept to her man. And with fear, anger and hunger she put her hands on his mouth and pushed with all the strength of rage . . . pushed. We were dying of hunger. We were crying from fear. The sounds of the soldiers were the sounds of victory and satisfaction. It was the sound of water, the taste of bread, meat. The hungry old man, under the hands of his sick, hungry wife, died. Death from two sides: up there, death from swords; down here, death from hunger.

The yells of drunken soldiers and neighs of satisfied horses shook us, who were unconscious, frightened and mad. The eyes, impudent, mad, hungry, savage eyes . . . our eyes . . . looked at each other. Hunger decreed. And with all the might of a hyena, a boar, a vulture, we stormed. The pieces of the old man's body became the delicious food of being alive. The old woman was crying and biting. We were eating savagely . . . getting fed. Over our heads the soldiers and horses were eating and drinking, glancing scornfully at the corpses of our men who were massacred.

## Scene Eleven

**Zahhak** *and the* **Devil** *start to whip the people, who try to escape towards the audience.*

**Narrator** So the King and the devil captured country after country, until their world-conquering army reached Kaveh's country, a country like other countries, with similar oppressed people and a similar negligent oppressor king and ministers who were ruling heedlessly.

## Scene Twelve

*The* **King***'s court. During this scene the rising sounds of the people can be heard, reaching a peak as the fighting gets closer to the palace.*

**Bugler** The great protector of the world, his most gracious Imperial Majesty, the King of Kings.

**King** Wise minister, how do our subjects and servants pass time in comfort?

**Minister** Praising your Imperial Majesty's justice and praying thankfully for your Imperial Majesty.

**King** Anyone dissatisfied?

**Minister** Impossible.

**King** Anyone oppressed?

**Minister** Impossible.

**King** Nowhere in the protectorates?

**Minister** As long as your Imperial Majesty is sitting on the throne of the empire, justice is spread over the inhabited quarter of the world. And blessed by your security, wolves and sheep live in brotherhood, lions and deer go sight-seeing round the plains hand in hand.

**King** (*pause*) What a boring profession. We are tired and bored with our heavy responsibilities. Hasn't anyone given gifts and presents, paid tolls and duties to our most blessed treasury?

**Minister** The governor of the southern countries has offered twenty camel loads of gold, asking for the lands around the royal gardens.

**King** Granted.

**Minister** The governor of the eastern countries has offered one thousand gold and two thousand silver coins, minted in India, asking for the heads of two criminals.

**King** Have we any? Which criminals?

**Minister** One has gathered guerrillas to revolt against the governor . . .

**King** And the other?

**Minister** He is an escapee judge who has refused the governor's orders to sentence an innocent man to death.

**King** One thousand gold and two thousand silver coins? For only two heads? Granted. (*Pause.*) Haven't we received any requests for help and compassionate loans from the other kings? Hasn't any government asked for our liberating army to help suppress the rise and revolt of their people?

*The sounds of the people reach a crescendo.*

**Minister** Frightened by your Imperial Majesty's victorious liberating army, no people, nowhere in the world, would even contemplate uprisings and revolutions . . .

**King** Any requests for our royal donation? Any news?

**Minister** I have received one unimportant request and I have news . . . for your Imperial Majesty.

**King** Good or bad?

**Minister** It is up to your Imperial Majesty to decide. A savage and uncivilized dragon king, who apparently doesn't know the war tactics, has entered the soil of your most powerful Imperial Majesty's country with his plundering army. And has even dared reach the gates of the Imperial palace.

**King** (*fearfully*) Then we decide the news is bad. But doesn't this savage, uncivilized dragon king say what he requests?

**Minister** He has only one unimportant request: he wants the Imperial crown and the throne.

**King** A shameless, an insolent king! Why do you say he is savage . . . and uncivilized?

**Minister** He has two snakes on his shoulders.

**King** Very dangerous. In our royal opinion fighting such a monster is below our dignity and status. It is best to grant him the unimportant things he has requested . . .

*They both run away.*

# Act Two

Scene One

*A public place. The* **Herald** *blows a trumpet, calling the people together. The people gather round the* **Herald**.

**Herald** Attention . . . attention . . .

You heroic and brave people, attention. This announcement has just been made by the headquarters of war and the council for martial law:

Fellow countrymen, the troops of tyranny, which had dominated you, are crushed by our troops of friendship. Your king, who for years encroached on your belongings, lives and dignity, together with his traitor collaborators, has chosen escape over resistance. Congratulations and greetings to you, who from today will live under a king who has no worries and thoughts other than equality and brotherhood, a king who will liberate all the world.

The royal policy for security, health and the provision of public needs is as follows:
One: The gathering of people, more than two, strictly forbidden.
Two: Spreading slogans against the victorious regime, strictly forbidden.
Three: Carrying illegal arms, strictly forbidden.
Four: Leaving your homes after sundown, strictly forbidden.
Five: Reading unofficial leaflets and night-letters, strictly forbidden.
Offenders will be punished by death.

Also you, the hard-working people, are strictly required to submit whatever foodstuffs you have at home, in shops or on farms, to the officials. Whatever cash, gold or jewellery you have saved submit immediately to the officials. So in this manner you take part in securing your share in public needs, health and security. It is clear that the discovery of anyone in possession of the mentioned stuffs and objects, wherever they may be, is evidence of the owner's treachery and will be punished by death.

The New King's Advisor,
The Prime Minister of the Victorious King,
The Commander of the World Conquering Army,
The Commander of Martial Law in the Country,
The Minister of Your Finance,
Lord Merchant. (*He bows.*)

Scene Two

*A public house.*

**Narrator** And the snakes on the king's shoulders . . . the gifts of the devil's kisses . . . and the king and the devil are ruling the people . . . the oppressed people . . . the people who are the creators of history and life. The objectors, the people-lovers, from worker to peasant, from teacher to student, are taken to prisons and execution yards. And the world, that is to say the world usurped by kings and devils . . . and snakes . . . is turning around this orbit . . . the orbit that sooner or later will be ruined by the cancer of corruption.

**A Man** The King has appointed governors . . . and the governors are ruling over our life and dignity. The land that is the land of the people is usurped by them, and the peasants who are the fathers of the land are their slaves and bonds-men. The workshops that were made by the able hands of the people have become the factories to tie them. The governors and the rich are dancing over the corpses of the history-makers, with the throats of strugglers in their grasp.

**A Woman** Like snakes . . . like dragons . . . they swallow and become corpulent. And their poison spreads death in the blood of the people, in the veins of society, in the hearts of the cities.

People! I am talking to you . . . I have given up all hope of my life, for I know that in lieu of this truth, I will be the bait for the king's snakes. No one will come to your rescue, there is no hope for a miracle. You people, rescue yourselves . . . be your own miracle.

*The soldiers break the door in and enter.*

**Soldiers** You are under arrest.

## Scene Three

*A prison. The prisoners, under the lashes of the whip are turning a big, heavy wheel around in the circle.*

**A Prisoner**  The roses of our land are hunted by the gales.
The roses of our rage are rotting in the jails.
Dawn is gloomy in execution yards,
For the heroes of the people face the ruler's guards.
The roses of our lands, oh peasant and worker,
Destroy the oppression, cruelty and torture.
Oh worker and peasant, the roses of our lands,
You history-makers, the world is in your hands.


## Scene Four

*A public house.*

**A Man**  It's true she was my wife, for fourteen full years, but well . . . what would you do if you were me? First, my foreman called me, 'Watch your wife'. My back twinged. Then my employer said, 'Come to my office.' I thought perhaps he had noticed why something went missing every week. I went in. He said, 'A man's wife is a man's dignity. If you don't watch your wife, you are dismissed.' I asked forty-eight hours' leave. He said, 'Go'. I said, 'With pay?' He said, 'I said go'.

What would you do if you were me? I chased her for two full days. When she left the workshop in the afternoon I chased her from shadow to shadow. In two days, not with one, not with two . . . guess with how many? I saw her with four different men. They met cautiously, they whispered, letters were exchanged, then a fast departure. The second day when she left the workshop she started running. I ran too. It looked as though she was late. I was breathless when she reached a ruined house and stopped. I stopped too. She looked around. I pulled myself behind the wall . . . one, two, three. I glanced quickly. Side by side together with a skinny young man, she turned into the ruined house. What would you do if you were me?

I reached the ruined house. Blood covered my eyes. I went in, but it seemed they had vanished into the ground like water. Search here, search there . . . no luck. What would you do if you were me? I went home. I waited for one hour, two hours, three hours. Just about nightfall she appeared, carrying a full bag. Mercilessly I slapped her in the face . . . once, twice, three times. Punching was to follow. I beat her, blood all over her, but she didn't cry, didn't shout. I beat her until she fell unconscious. What would you do if you were me?

I took the bag, I opened it. My heart stopped . . . treachery . . . after fourteen years. So whatever they say is true. It was all in the bag. I took the bag and straightaway went to my employer's house. I said, 'Forty-eight hours are up and this is the evidence to prove what a tractable worker I am.' My employer put his hand in his pocket and put this many notes in my hand, saying 'One of these days you will be a foreman.' I kissed his hand. I ran towards the bar. What would you do if you were me, if after fourteen years, you find out that your wife is trying to unite the workers?

Since they have taken her, I haven't had any news from her. It's true she was my wife, but well . . . what would you do if you were me?

## Scene Five

*The execution yard. Two soldiers execute the prisoner who was singing in the prison.*

## Scene Six

*In the streets. The people carry the corpse on their shoulders, mourning. They reach the palace.* **Zahhak** *and the* **Devil** *are upstage.*

**Devil** Your Majesty, apparently some people have gathered in front of the royal palace, who desire your Imperial Majesty's attention.

**Zahhak** Some people? What attention do they desire?

**Devil** (*to the people*) What do you desire?

**First Man** We are the people's representatives . . . workers and peasants . . . we have complaints against the governors and ministers. We plead for justice.

**Devil**  Your Majesty, the representatives of the workers and peasants have come to plead for justice.

**Zahhak**  What about?

**Devil**  They have complaints against the governors and ministers.

**Zahhak**  Only against them?

**Zahhak**  *approaches the people, and motions for them to sit.*

**First Man**  We are the people . . . people who have had enough harrassment from your appointed governors and agents.

**First Woman**  They kill our men.

**Second Man**  They take our women by force.

**Third Man**  And they plunder the harvests of our labour.

**Zahhak**  The land has laws, doesn't it?

**Second Man**  The law is written by them.

**Zahhak**  By them? The law is written by us.

**Second Woman**  And it is written against us.

**Devil**  (*interrupts*)  Ruling the country needs money. Who will ensure the expenses?

**Zahhak**  Rulers or people?

**Devil**  People. The country needs sacrificing. Who must make sacrifices?

**Zahhak**  Rulers or people?

**Devil**  People.

**Second Man**  Who reaps the benefits of our labour? Us or the rulers?

**People**  Not us.

**Third Woman**  Who imprisons our freedom to shed our blood freely? Us or the rulers?

**People**  Not us.

**Fourth Woman**  We are at our wit's end. There is no house in the land that is not in mourning for a young martyr . . .

**Fourth Man**  There is no pasture, no village, that is not crushed under the cruelty of soldiers.

**Devil**  Your rudeness is beyond limit.

**First Woman**  Your tyranny is beyond limit.

**Third Man**  You have plundered our minds and lands by force . . .

**Third Woman**  And our share is nothing but work, poverty, illness and fear.

**Devil**  In return we have defended your land from the enemies.

**Fourth Woman**  The enemies of our land are your friends, for the victims are the workers and peasants from both sides, not the rulers.

**Second Man**  The land is all anger . . .

**First Man**  Ready to burst.

**Fourth Woman**  Pull out the roots of injustice or we will.

**Zahhak**  We? Who are you?

**First Woman**  I am Kaveh the blacksmith.

**Second Man**  I am Kaveh the blacksmith.

**Third Woman**  I am Kaveh the blacksmith.

**Fourth Woman**  I am Kaveh the blacksmith.

**Second Man**  I am Kaveh the blacksmith.

**Zahhak**  You provoke our anger . . . and face horrible punishment.

**First Woman**  Which punishment is more horrible than living under the shadow of injustice?

**Third Woman**  When our loved ones are the bait for your snakes.

**Fourth Woman**  When your prisons are full of our youngsters.

**Second Man**  Then which punishment are you giving us?

**Devil**  I warn you that you tempt death.

**First Man**  We live a death. We are not frightened of death, but of living with death.

**Third Woman**  We have come as the people's representatives, to warn you that if the government doesn't know the rights of the people, the people will find a solution themselves.

**Zahhak**  People? The cowered, illiterate beggars? Empty-handed creatures? Make these smelly useless bodies the target of arrows and spears!

*The soldiers shoot the people.*


Scene Seven

*The royal court.*

**Narrator**  And the snakes on the king's shoulders, when hungry would make him suffer so much that the whole world would become hell in his eyes. But when fed on the brains of the people, the world would turn to paradise.

*The snakes are hungry. They start to torment the **King**. They writhe around his neck. The **King** cries out and falls down. The **Devil** is watching him. The **King**, falling and rising, reaches the **Devil** and holds his feet.*

**Zahhak**  (*entreatingly*)  The snakes are killing me.

**Devil**  They are hungry.

**Zahhak**  They are killing me, don't you see?

**Devil**  They won't. The King is safe. They only want you to feed them.

**Zahhak**  I already did.

**Devil**  Not enough.

**Zahhak**  I beg you to help me. I will do anything you order. Just relieve me from the evil of the snakes.

**Devil**  How can I? They are yours; they are with you; they are you.

**Zahhak**  Cut them. Kill them.

**Devil**  They are your honour, your essence. The snakes are your miracle.

**Zahhak** Just cut them, I beg you. The King is begging you.

**Devil** Touching the royal belongings is an unforgivable sin.

**King** Cut them, you devil!

**Devil** Cutting the royal flags is a terrible crime, your Majesty.

**Zahhak** (*angrily*) We, the Most Gracious Imperial Majesty, the King of Kings, command you. This is an imperial charter. I beg you!

**Devil** I obey you, your Majesty.

*The **Devil** cuts the snakes from the **King**'s shoulders.*

*The **King** screams. The **Devil** laughs.*

**Narrator** But the snakes were the evil seeds of the oath, and grew again and again. And, like the snakes, the more the King killed and the more he ate, the more greedy he got.

Scene Eight

*A public place.*

**A Young Man** From cell to cell, from block to block, the news went round, 'political prisoners will be freed'. An old woman, who was imprisoned as a youth, on seeing the image of a river, hearing a child's laugh, cried. A man who had never seen his five-year-old daughter, collected the dolls that he had made from dough, dolls of different sizes and faces but with one name, the name of his daughter.

The older prisoners were trying to recall the names of the streets, their friends and to remember their own faces, and the time too: which day of the week it was, which week of which month . . .

When the news went round, generosity followed: cigarette butts out of mattresses, rusty files out of crevices, broken pencil ends, pieces of newspaper were brought out. The dearest presents in the world were spread among the prisoners; and then a song went round from block to block, from cell to cell:

'Freedom . . . freedom . . . man must be free.

The devil has made prisons to defeat God.'

The political prisoners were looking at each other happily,
seeing the faces of their beloved: Are they alive? Are they well:
Have they stayed? Are they free? Do they remember us? The
people . . . people . . . it must be their force. This must be the
people's will and power to force the jailers to free the
prisoners. Outside, there must be something happening,
something good.

And that night wasn't the night of sleep, wasn't the night of
torture, wasn't the night of the fear of tomorrow. It wasn't the
last night of a prisoner's life. It was the last night, the last night
of being imprisoned. In the morning, from block to block,
from cell to cell, political prisoners were called by name. Kisses
and tears of farewell. The kisses of those who were remaining
and the tears of those who were leaving.

Line by line in queues, they took them from prison to freedom.
And freedom was a field surrounded by soldiers ready to
shoot. A field under the feet of the political prisoners, who,
angry and tricked, were running and yelling. A field that was
captured by the execution order. And the news went round
from cell to cell, from block to block.

Scene Nine

*The bazaar. The people are working, when a corpse is carried in.*

**Narrator** Slaughter . . . after slaughter, injustice after injustice.
Girl and boy, man and woman, young and old . . . are not
immune to the King's massacre. Anyone who says 'no' to the
continuation of injustice has said 'yes' to death by the
executioner. The young birds fall down so the old snakes can
continue their poisonous lives . . .

**First Man** The malicious, blood-thirsty man who has taken the
sovereign throne sheds our and our children's blood to the last
drop. He taxes us more heavily, and scornfully laughs at our
faith and beliefs. You people have yourselves witnessed how
many sons of mine alone he has martyred; each a fresh sapling,
each a newly-lit light. You have yourselves witnessed how I sat
in mourning in the middle of this bazaar; how we sat in
mourning in the middle of this bazaar.

**Second Man** If anyone has an Arabian horse, swift-footed and long-maned, he calls it his own and takes it by force.

**First Woman** If any man has a woman, fair and beautiful, he takes her in lust and gallops away.

**Third Man** Friends! My back is broken under the heavy taxes. I am all alone. What if I had a horse, swift-footed and long-maned; what if I had a woman, fair and beautiful; what if I had sons?

**Second Woman** Each day in war with a neighbour, each day submitting to a plague, each day obeying a new law. Where is the Goddess of Death to reign over our bodies, so that our souls might descend upon other bodies in another land?

**First Man** Humble fellow-sufferers! Broken-hearted fellow-mourners! Neither have we the leisure to submit more than we have, nor are we reprieved to sit and cry. Neither can we stay and watch, nor can we set our hearts on migration. There is no escape in submitting to slavery and poverty in the hope of death. And there is no salvation in remaining in silence and giving in to the existing injustice. We are the same people who, with unarmed, wounded hands, send bread to his colourful table from the wild hungry lands. We are the same people who die in the damp workshops, to make clothes for his evil, stinking body. We are the same people who burn our sweating faces, forging tempered swords to decorate his fat waist. We are the same . . . and if we remain the same . . . it will always be the same.

**Third Man** If you have a chosen way in mind . . .

**First Man** I have.

**Third Woman** If it is possible to sit joyfully round the bread-cloth just once, without fear of the dawn . . .

**First Man** It is.

**Second Man** Then tell! My heart is lonesome for a home in which the wailing of a child breaks its dreadful silence, a child that is mine.

**First Man** We shall rise together, with bare hands, bare feet, bare chests; and we will destroy him, for there is no time to delay.

**Fourth Woman**  His guards and soldiers will kill us all!

**Fourth Man**  Our bodies will become the target for arrows and spears, and our beloved ones will become the homeless weepers in our dirge, for whose destiny the stones of the desert will cry.

**First Man**  Frightened ignorants . . . is it not so now? We have seen the death of our beloved ones with our own eyes, in whose mourning we cried like the winter cloud. Have we not seen the sliced bodies of our brothers and sisters hanging off the piles? And will we not see it again? Once is our death and until death we live. For us, the captives of oppression, sweet is the liberating death I choose and you fear.

*He opens his apron and ties it to a stick that someone gives him. He starts marching toward the palace and the people follow him.*

**Zahhak**  I am frightened . . . say something.

**Devil**  There is nothing to be afraid of, your Majesty. Be easy and courageous . . . your Imperial Majesty must not be afraid of anyone or anything. You have everything, and the people have nothing, not even graves. Has your Imperial Majesty forgotten his wealth and power?

**Zahhak**  No, of course not. I have swift-footed horses . . . I have beautiful women . . . wealth . . . armies . . . palaces . . . hunting grounds. I love hunting

**Devil**  Yes, your Majesty, you have them, and the snakes, too.

**Zahhak**  And I'm frightened . . . the snakes are hungry.

*The people enter the palace, find **Zahhak** and the **Devil** and kill them.*


Scene Ten

You do not know,
when the bullets sing,
how the chests bloom,
how hearts blossom,
how death blows,
and
how El Salvador cries.
You do not know,
and
I love you.

You do not know,
when the tanks tread,
how hands become strong-holds,
for hearts to sing one yell more,
under the iron feet.
And
how streets
are the grave-yards of yells
in Cambodia.
You do not know,
and
I love you.

You do not know,
when hunger gallops in,
how sisters submit
their red flowers of virginity
to the viciousness of soldiers' sickles.
For their brothers
to join the winds of homelessness
on the horses of the night
from the blown shelters.
And
how the bastard infants
are thirsty for the blood
of their fathers,
in Eritrea.
You do not know,
and
I love you.

You do not know,
how they shoot the god
to frighten the devils.
How they behead the flowers
and brand the doves.
How the blood of oil
congeals in the veins of greed.
How the trees turn into gallows
and hands into whips.
And
how Iran is cut into pieces
under the cleaver of fear.

You do not know,
and
I love you.

You do not know,
how they hunt
the hungry children,
to sell fat boars
more dearly to the zoos.
How they castrate men,
for white masters
to buy chastity belts
for their wives.
And
how black Africa
burns and becomes red.
You do not know,
and
I love you.

You do not know,
while they were cutting
the heart of Kurdestan into pieces
with the sword of tyranny,
how the flowers of Chile
fell to dust, blood-stained.
How the songs of Vietnam's canaries
became red,
and
how love flapped to death
in Argentina.
You do not know,
and
I love you.

You do not know,
Irans,
Eritreas,
Cambodias,
El Salvadors,
are the same bazaar,
built by old merchants,
for you
to pass through every day
to sell your youth.

You do not know,
and
I love you.

For I know
that your arms,
one day
will hide me,
who shivers from
the torture of knowing.
And you
will shout 'cry for the world'
with the blood-stained voice.
You do not know,
and
I love you.

# Prometheus in Evin

*For Clive Doig*

**Promethus in Evin** was first performed in Farsi at The Royal Court Theatre Upstairs on 2 July 1987 with the following cast:

| | |
|---|---|
| **Woman**<br>**Woman In Chains**<br>**Escapee** | Soudabeh Farrokhnia |
| **Guard** | Hamid Haghighat |
| **1st Interrogator**<br>**Guard**<br>**Mortician** | Ali Kamrani |
| **Man**<br>**Guard** | Nasser Memarzia |
| **2nd Interrogator**<br>**Guard** | Akbar Moein |
| **3rd Interrogator**<br>**Guard** | Yousef Nikpour |
| **Guard**<br>**Mortician Assistant** | Sia Rahmany |

*Directed by* Iraj Jannatie Ataie
*Designed by* Ali Allen

The play was performed in English at The Young Vic Studio on 3 October 1988 with the following cast:

| | |
|---|---|
| **Woman**<br>**Woman in Chains**<br>**Escapee** | Soudabeh Farrokhnia |
| **Man** | Anthony Allen |
| **Guard** | Ivan Steward |
| **1st Interrogator** | Kulvinder Ghir |
| **2nd Interrogator** | Kwabino Manso |
| **3rd Interrogator** | Johnny Myers |
| **Tied Woman**<br>**Contact** | Pamela Nomvete |
| **TV Interviewer** | Nigel Hughes |
| **Mortician** | Jimmie Wheels |
| **Youth** | Nico Brown |
| **Fugitive** | Kumi Liley |
| **1st Agent** | Aidan Dooley |
| **2nd Agent** | Michael Andrus |
| **Guards, Mourners etc.** | Stephen Daltry, Giles Newington, Andrew Rose |

*Directed by* Phil Young
*Designed by* Ann Haworth and Penny Fitt

## Scene One

*The sitting room.*

**Man** *is sitting on a chair. His chest is bare.* **Woman** *is standing behind him, drying his hair with a hairdryer, humming a popular song.*

**Man**  I am a poet. I haven't got a choice. (*Pause.*) This is my job. My life. (*Pause.*) Why don't you come? Participate? Or just listen – you used to.

*He tries to hold her hands but she draws back.*

I care about the people. (*Pause.*) We only talk.

*The telephone rings.* **Woman** *stops.* **Man** *stands holding the hairdryer, carries on drying his hair.* **Woman** *goes to the phone.*

**Man**  If it's them, say I've already left.

**Woman**  (*picks up the phone*)  Hello? Hello? (*Puts the phone down.*)

**Man**  Who was it?

**Woman**  Don't know.

**Man**  What?

**Woman**  It was cut off.

**Man**  What?

**Woman**  Cut off.

**Man**  (*alarmed*)  Cut off? Was it a man or woman?

**Woman**  It was cut off.

*The telephone rings. They remain still. The phone rings.* **Man** *drops the hairdryer on the table, rushing towards the phone. He picks up the receiver.*

**Man**  Hello. Hello? Yes. Speaking.

*Gestures to her to turn the hairdryer off. She does so.*

Hello. Yes. That is very kind of you. (*Pause.*) But I am not a journalist, I'm a . . . Hello? Hello? (*He puts the phone down, scared.*) It's time, I guess. Yes, it's time.

**Woman**  What?

**Man**  The committee.

**Woman** (*whispers*) Committee?

**Man** (*frightened*) I'm cold. Funny in this weather.

*Starts to put his shirt on.* **Woman** *helps him fearfully.*

I already miss you.

**Woman** You've got to leave.

**Man** Where?

**Woman** Ring someone.

**Man** (*putting his shoes on*) Who?

*Door bell. Silence. Door bell.*

**Woman** I'm afraid.

*Door bell.*

**Man** Open it.

**Woman** Is it them?

*The couple are frozen. The door is being kicked.* **Woman** *goes towards the door slowly and opens it. Three men come in. One of them is carrying a big brief case. Two of them bring their pistols out and the third brings a light machine-gun out of his brief case. Very quickly they move to different corners of the room with their weapons pointed at the couple.*

**1st Interrogator** Don't be afraid. This is a routine check. (*Looking around.*) How many rooms do you have?

**Man** Two.

**1st Interrogator** Telephone?

**Man** One.

**1st Interrogator** (*orders the armed men to search the flat, with a gesture*) Don't be afraid.

**Woman** What are you looking for?

**1st Interrogator** Dangerous things. Rubbish.

**Woman** What has he done?

**1st Interrogator** Don't be afraid. (*He picks up the phone and dials.*) Hello, workshop? We're ready to return with the materials. (*Puts the phone down. To* **Man**.) I have orders to take you with me for questioning. Don't be afraid.

*One of the armed men comes in from his search carrying a sack full of manuscripts and notebooks. Puts it down in front of* **1st Interrogator** *He looks in it.*

**Man** What is the charge?

**1st Interrogator** Only a few questions. Don't be afraid.

**Woman** How long will it take?

**1st Interrogator** Forty-five minutes to an hour. I'll bring him back myself. Don't be afraid.

*Two secret policemen take the* **Man** *between them and push him towards the door.* **1st Interrogator** *follows them.* **Woman** *takes* **Man**'s *cigarettes and matches. Running to the door, shouting.*

**Woman** Wait . . .

**1st Interrogator** *turns back and hits her in the stomach with the butt of machine-gun, hard. The* **Woman** *writhes and moans with pain and then falls on the floor.*

*Lights fade to blackout.*


Scene Two

**Man** *is standing downstage, bloody and breathless. A spotlight is on him.*

**Man** Red Mercedes. Yellow Toyota.

In all their mourning, the streets seemed lively and liberated. The taste of fear had dried my mouth. In the depths of my heart a spider was weaving threads of ice; spinning them throughout my body. A guard blindfolded me to darkness. I was in a sweat and the Mercedes' windows barred the fresh air.

The Committee building. Humiliation. Waiting. Foul words. Body search. Beating. Waiting. Queue of detainees. Beating. Blood. Fear. Machine-gun. Pistol. Sobbing. Sighing. Pride. Hope. Anxiety. Waiting . . . Waiting . . . The committee chief. Questions. Silence. Slap. Questions. Phone call. Guards. Blindfold. Darkness. Beating. Degradation. Being thrown into the corridor. Off the stairs. Squeezed into a car. Sound of speed.

Two hands from my left and right were pushing my head toward my knees. Bumps in the road on the left, on the right. Braking. Squeaking of an iron gate. Moving again. Brakes. Forceful exit and . . . my scream. All the mountains of the world fell upon my shoulders in the butt of a machine-gun. Cry of pain. Despair! The black tremor. Unconsciousness . . .

It was raining. A cool breeze of feeling. The odorous rain of a bucket of blood and water which they poured over my head.

Consciousness. Light. The blindfold was removed. I was spread over a metal bed. There were stone walls and chains as far as the eye could see. The absence of a window reminded me of fear.

Automatically I moved to embrace my knees and hide my face between my arms. The handcuffs on my wrists and the iron bed. The handcuffs on my ankles and the iron bed.

And the sting of wire cables on my bare feet. And the cracking sound of splitting skin and flesh. And the non-stop barrage of unending questions. My bloodied lips were torn between my teeth.

Silence. Whizzing cables. Questions. Silence. Pain. Pain.

Mixture of blood and water.
Awakening pain. My scream.
A guard pushes a rotten rag into my mouth.
Nausea.
Suffocation.
My bulging eyes.
Handcuffs removed. Hands and feet freed. (*Pause.*)
No. That was not the end of that tunnel of absolute solitude.
Turned over. Handcuffs return.
Someone with the heaviness of a giant jumped and sat on my back.
Feeling of nakedness.
Sound of ripping flesh.
And the descent of whip-lashes on the bare back of a human being – who is me.
Who was me.
Tarantulas. Tarantulas all over me.

Numbness.

Confusion.

Sleeplessness.

Seven times eight . . . Nine times seven . . .

Nausea.

Capital of Zambia? . . . Birth-year of Khayam? The main export of Britain?

Dizziness and pain. Weightlessness.

And slowly I was beginning to move away from the bed, from the gaol, from the Earth and myself.

Amidst the lashes someone roared behind my back –

'Dirty dog . . . filthy jam rag'

I went further and further away from the world.

What goes on in your frightened mind?

Who is this perplexed woman? Mother?

I'm thirsty, my wife.

My sister remains by the curtains, still looking at the street.

Whose tall shadow is this? Father why are you depressed?

My brother is singing in the yard.

Where is my son?

When I came to, I was a mound of flesh wrapped in straps of pain, bundled up in the corner of a prison cell full of other flesh mounds.

Day or night? Dawn or dusk – of which day or night?

Who am I?

Who was I?

*Lights fade to blackout.*


## Scene Three

*The interrogation room.*

*An old steel desk and two chairs are on each side.* **Man** *is sitting on one of them. Behind him there is a* **Guard** *watching. The sound of whipping and moaning can be heard from outside. The sack of books is in the corner.* **Man** *is blindfolded.*

**Man**  Am I allowed to smoke? (*No reply.*) Can you give me a cigarette?

*The* **Guard** *does not answer. After a while* **Man** *puts his head between his hands and his elbows on the table, and thinks. The* **Guard** *hits him on the shoulder with the butt of his rifle.* **Man** *crumples with pain.*

**Guard** No sleeping!

**Man** I wasn't sleeping. I was thinking.

**Guard** Well don't think!

**Man** Alright.

*The door opens and the* **Interrogator** *enters. He carries a black brief-case. He gestures. The* **Guard** *leaves the room. He sits on a chair stage right. Opens the brief-case, takes out a small mirror, a pair of scissors and a comb, setting them on the desk and starts to trim his moustache.*

**2nd Interrogator** Now then, it's my job to get you and your sort nicely 'prepared' for their interrogation. (*Pause. Looking in the mirror.*) Contrary to popular belief the tools of my trade are very simple.

*He takes a leather belt out of his case. Hits him on the shoulder, hard.* **Man** *crumples.*

Do you think I'll let scum like you get me into trouble?

**Man** I . . .

**2nd Interrogator** Don't talk. This place is for pain and crying. So – you're allowed to shout – cry – beg. (*Hits him.*)

**Man** Why are you hitting me?

*The* **Interrogator** *stands up, takes the* **Man** *by his blindfold and makes him stand, then pushes him around.*

**2nd Interrogator** Look mate, I've done the 'preparing' on plenty of people today and I am shagged out. Besides, I quite like you. You're different to the rest. As soon as I read your file I recognized you, my daughter's a big fan of yours. And that is why I am being soft on you. But I am only going to be, if you make it easy for me.

**Man** How?

**2nd Interrogator** Shut up you son of a bitch. (*Pause.*) Do you want to be beaten up? (*No reply.*) I asked if you wanted to be beaten up?

**Man** *is not certain whether to reply.* **Interrogator** *pushes him around harder.*

Answer me you bastard.

**Man**  No.

**2nd Interrogator**  Excellent, then we will make a little deal. You don't want to be beaten up and I am too tired to do the beating, but we need a little bit of noise to show I'm doing my job properly.

**Man**  I don't get you.

**2nd Interrogator**  What kind of an intellectual are you? Look thickhead, I am knackered, but I've got to get you ready for interrogation, and it is a noisy business getting you ready. Now, you don't want to be beaten up? So you can do my job as well as yours but instead of hitting yourself, hit the door, the wall whatever you like . . . But shout, cry . . . Scream with pain. Get it?

**Man**  Yes but . . .

**2nd Interrogator**  No buts, you mother fucker. Get on with it before I change my mind.

*The* **Interrogator** *puts the belt in* **Man**'s *hand.* **Man** *starts lashing the air, uncertainly.*

**Man**  Why?

**2nd Interrogator**  Harder. Groan, shout, cry, yell.

**Man** *beats harder and his voice picks up. The* **Interrogator** *brings out some sheets of paper and a pen from his brief-case.*

**2nd Interrogator**  Have you got a wife?

**Man**  Yes.

**2nd Interrogator**  Louder you bastard, and don't stop beating, the noise mustn't stop.

**Man** *continues.* **Interrogator** *writes something down.*

Got any children?

**Man**  Yes.

**2nd Interrogator**  One?

**Man**  Yes.

**2nd Interrogator**  Is the flat yours?

**Man**  No.

**2nd Interrogator**  Any relative living abroad?

**Man**  Yes.

**Woman**  Anyone in the army?

**Man**  Yes.

**2nd Interrogator**  Who's your leader?

**Man**  No one.

**2nd Interrogator**  Who do you get your orders from?

**Man**  No one.

**2nd Interrogator**  Louder. Harder. Is your wife involved too?

**Man**  (*stops beating. Shouts*)  In what?

**2nd Interrogator**  Beat you pimp.

**Man**  She was always busy with her work.

**2nd Interrogator**  Does she know what you've been up to? Does she?

**Man**  I haven't done anything.

**2nd Interrogator**  Beat.

**Man**  We just used to get together, read poems, talk.

**2nd Interrogator**  Shout louder. So you used to 'get together'? Talk? What about your wife?

**Man**  She got fed up with it.

**2nd Interrogator**  Who was in the group?

**Man**  What group?

**2nd Interrogator**  Beat you son of a bitch. The 'discussion group'. Who are the organizers?

**Man**  We only used to . . .

**2nd Interrogator**  Who?

**Man**  It was different every time. People used to come and go. I don't remember.

**2nd Interrogator**  Don't worry. You'll remember. We'll make you remember.

**Man**   I am only an intellectual!

**2nd Interrogator**   What is your organisation called? What is your part in it all?

**Man** (*beats the wall and himself, shouting*)   I'm only an intellectual!

**2nd Interrogator**   Are you? Son of a bitch. You are or you were? (*Laughs.*)

OK! That's enough. By the way . . . can I have your autograph for my daughter?

*Lights fade to blackout.*


Scene Four

*The sitting room.*

**Woman** *is alone, walking around, smoking a cigarette. Sits. Listening to* **Man***'s voice reciting the* Prometheus *poem which can be heard from the tape recorder. She thinks and cries quietly.*

**Man's Voice**   And since;
The poorest God of Gods
      – Prometheus
Became aware, that
People
    – The proud suffering hosts
In search of the mystery of fire,
       – The enlightening liberator
In the oppressive purgatory of Gods
       – The few cruel tyrants
Under the hail of constant injustice,
In the authority of coldness,
     – Snow,
      – And ice-storms
Are convicted,
    – Destroyed.
He freed the distinct secret of fire,
From the dreadful prison of the
      – Evil Gods.
And scattered the red seed of fire,
On the people's frozen land.

And since Prometheus was
                    – The poorest God of Gods;

*The phone rings. She picks up the receiver and puts it back to cut it off.*

In the court of injustice,
He was condemned:
                    To be bound
                              – To be tortured
                    – To suffer,
Condemned to exile
Exile to the heart of earth;
Until the last tomorrow.
And from dawn to sundown
The tamed torturers of deceiving Gods
                              – The blind

          – Liver-eating
Vultures
Were to get fat and drunk on the human Prometheus'
Liver
              And blood,
At each dawn.

*The phone rings again. She cuts it off.*

So that he
          – Prometheus, the prisoner of time
May believe,
How alone he is left,
How defeated he is left.
But Prometheus . . .

*Someone is knocking at the door. She goes to the tape recorder, turns it off. Puts a scarf on her head. Goes towards the door, and opens it.* **1st Interrogator** *enters.* **Woman** *walks away backwards.* **1st Interrogator** *comes forward with a friendly smile on his face.* **Woman** *is standing uncertainly.* **1st Interrogator** *is inspecting the room now.*

**1st Interrogator**  Are you alone?

**Woman**  Yes.

**1st Interrogator**  Where is the kid?

**Woman**  At my mother's.

**1st Interrogator**  Good. (*Sits.*) If the boys find out that I am here . . .

**Woman**  What do you want?

**1st Interrogator**  Listen, I am taking a risk. I've come to tell you something.

**Woman**  Tell me what?

**1st Interrogator**  Ever since the day we came to arrest your husband, I've felt sorry for you . . . So . . . I thought . . . I might be able to help you.

**Woman**  What do you want?

**1st Interrogator**  Look, your husband needs help. You've got to help him.

**Woman**  You think I've been sitting around doing nothing? I've tried everybody. I've written to everybody, but the answers are all the same. 'There's nothing we can do.' 'He wouldn't have been arrested if he wasn't guilty'. 'You'll just have to wait.' (*Pause.*) What can I do all by myself, on my own?

**1st Interrogator**  You are just a woman. You can't do anything. Especially if you lose your man. (*Pause.*) If you don't do something to help him it'll be even worse. If they prove that your husband is a hypocrite or a communist he'll lose his rights to all his property, including his wife, before getting killed!

**Woman**  But he hasn't done anything.

**1st Interrogator**  There is no need for you to worry. I said I've come to help you. But if you want to make my job easier, you'll have to confess.

**Woman**  Confess what?

**1st Interrogator**  Names of his friends – dates – anything.

**Woman**  The same old questions.

**1st Interrogator** (*goes to her*)  So you don't want to help him.

**Woman**  I'd do anything to help him. I'd give you anything you want if only you'll release him.

**1st Interrogator** (*caresses her hair*)  Anything?

**Woman** *draws back. The phone rings.*

Say you'd rather be left alone. Say you don't want any visitors. Tell them you don't want to talk about it, then put the phone down. Got it?

**Woman** *goes to the phone.* **1st Interrogator** *follows her. She picks up the phone, he holds his ear close to the receiver.*

**Woman**  Hello. Yes. No. No. Nothing new.

*The secret policeman gradually puts his arms round her waist. She draws back.*

No. (*Into the phone.*) I don't feel well. No. Later.

*She drops the receiver.* **1st Interrogator** *replaces it and comes on.*

No. Please! I have a husband and a child.

**1st Interrogator** (*tries to hug her*)  They both need your help.

**Woman**  I'll do whatever you say. I'll give anything you want. Please – I beg you.

*She tries to escape. They both struggle.*

**1st Interrogator**  Do you want your man back or don't you? You aren't going to lose much, are you? Nobody is here, just the two of us – I promise I'll release him for you, I swear to God I will.

**Woman** (*struggles*)  No. Please. I'll do whatever I can, I swear.

**1st Interrogator**  Having some fun with me is the best thing you can do.

**Woman**  No.

*Half naked, sweating, full of anger and fear she runs downstage, staying there, facing the audience. Lights go down. Only one spotlight on* **Woman**.

I've trailed across the whole city. I've pleaded with everyone I know. I've tried every official I can think of, but all the answers are the same. 'There's nothing we can do in this particular case!' In this 'particular case'. When a person opens his eyes and protests at what he sees, they become what officials call 'a particular case'. A particular case which spreads fear in the family, in the community and ends up with lives destroyed. (*Pause.*) I miss the moments I could have held him and I didn't; I could have helped him and I didn't; I could have just listened to him – much more than I did, but I didn't. What are they doing to him? What is going to happen to him? And it's not just me asking this question. There are countless other women and men asking the very same question, in other houses, in other streets, other cities and countries. (*Pause.*) What is happening to our women and men? What is happening to us?

*Lights fade to blackout.*


## Scene Five

*Prison*

*Absolute darkness. Foot-falls on winter leaves. The sound of water running. The monotonous sound of birds. The feeling of walking in a big garden in Winter must be conveyed to the audience.*

**1st Voice**  Hold his shoulder. Be careful not to touch his unclean hand.

**Man's Voice**  It's still summer, yet it feels like winter.

**2nd Voice**  It's always like this here, you'll be staying, so you'll catch on.

**Man's Voice**  So it is always winter in prison?

**2nd Voice**  For the prisoner.

**1st Voice**  For the filthy hypocrites like you.

*The sound of walking continues. Silence. Two sharp whistles. A door squeaks open. The foot-falls of someone wearing boots on mosaic tiles. The sound of a door being opened.*

**2nd Voice**  Remove his blindfold.

*The lights come on.* **1st Interrogator** *is removing* **Man***'s blindfold and is standing next to him. This is a room in prison. Almost empty. There are some stools and one telephone.* **3rd Interrogator** *is sitting on a stool. There is a metal bed standing vertically, upstage right, from which a wounded prisoner hangs by handcuffs.*

**3rd Interrogator**  How are you 'comrade'?

**1st Interrogator**  Why are you so pale? From fear? Don't be afraid.

**3rd Interrogator**  Sit down.

**1st Interrogator**  You're finished, your file is one of those marked 'dangerous'.

**3rd Interrogator**  Sit down.

**1st Interrogator**  Don't be afraid. If you are lucky enough you'll get execution.

**Man**  Why? What have I done?

**3rd Interrogator**  Practices against the security of the state. Connections with terrorist groups. And a thousand other kinds of sabotage.

**1st Interrogator**  Yet he asks 'what have I done?'

**3rd Interrogator**  Sit down.

**1st Interrogator** (*pushing him to sit down*)  Sit down. (**Man** *sits on a stool.*)

**3rd Interrogator**  I am nobody here, but I can help you, if you want. I have always said, one should help the helpless.

**1st Interrogator** (*to* **Man**)  This brother is very helpful. But only if you know how to get on with him.

**Man**  But what is my crime?

**3rd Interrogator** (*points at the wounded prisoner*)  Do you know her?

**Man** (*who had been peering at the unconscious woman now and then, looks at her again*)  No.

**3rd Interrogator**  Sure?

**Man**  Yes.

**3rd Interrogator**  She's finished. She'll certainly be executed if she's not dead already.

**1st Interrogator**  She's been roughed up so much that she's vomiting blood.

**3rd Interrogator**  My style is of course different to others. I am against violence, though the confessions are bigger and better when you use violence.

**1st Interrogator** Because it's a question of flesh and bone, and whips and fire.

**3rd Interrogator** But I always act logically, the logic of two and two. It's good for everyone when someone confesses and says whatever the interrogator wants. One, the accused won't have a nervous breakdown. He will be less insulted, and will have less pain; also, he will not have the agony of keeping all the secrets. Two, his friends outside will be arrested sooner. They will be saved from their errors sooner, their case settled sooner and, of course, relieved of the fear of being caught, sooner. Well, will you confess?

**Man** Confess what?

**1st Interrogator** Everything.

**Man** I haven't done anything to confess.

*From behind,* **1st Interrogator** *forces his fingers into* **Man**'s *mouth and pulls to tear his mouth apart.*

**1st Interrogator** Look! We know everything from A to Z. But we want you to say it in your own words. This will help you in court, do you understand?

**3rd Interrogator** (*to* **1st Interrogator**) Could you leave us alone? Tell the guards not to let anyone in, until I say so.

**1st Interrogator** *leaves* **Man** *alone. Looks at the* **3rd Interrogator** *with anger. Leaves the room.* **3rd Interrogator** *lights two cigarettes. Gives one to the* **Man**.

**3rd Interrogator** Don't think I am a savage interrogator, in the most horrible political prison. I have a Ph.D. in philosophy. And I know that there are inequalities in society. But abolishing everything is not the way to deal with it, one must roll one's sleeves up and enter the ring. There is theft? Extortion? Pulling strings? Well don't allow it. You are educated, you are young. Well join the establishment, join the government, be appointed to some job, then you can stop the corruption officially and legally. Am I not right? You are a literary man, well go to the press, to the radio and television. You are a technician, go to factories, you are a scientist, go to universities, go and improve them. We even give letters of recommendation to anyone who says he is ready. We telephone people to get them jobs, to give them freedom to operate freely. (*Pause.*) Who gives you orders? Who do you work for?

**Man** (*puts his cigarette out*)  I don't belong to any group or . . .

**3rd Interrogator** (*smiles*)  So you work for us then?

**Man**  For you?

**3rd Interrogator**  You are in this system, you have to work and earn money to live. Well, imagine that you go to an office asking for a job, it has a governor, of course, you say 'Sir, would you please give me a job? I know how to do such and such a job.' He takes a look at you and a look at us, the system, if we give the nod, he says; 'Yes, you are welcome.' Otherwise he says, 'I'm sorry there are no vacancies at the moment'. You will go to another office, another company, another organisation. Anyway, if they give you a job somewhere, it means we, the system, have given you the job. Is that clear?

**Man**  But there are millions of people working . . .

**3rd Interrogator**  Yes, but I am talking about the people who are important to the system. You become important to the system when you want to stand against it. Otherwise you don't count, and if you don't count you're a part of the system.

**Man**  What about those who stand against it?

**3rd Interrogator**  Maniacs. The question of a few revolutionaries is not an important problem.

**Man**  But you're calling them important!

**3rd Interrogator**  They have their own long or short-term importance. Long-term means excecution. You'll be of long-term importance to the system, when you're executed. And your short-term importance depends on the length of the time you take to become a part of the system. Is that clear? If you think of doing something not to be executed, you've started to become a part of the system and when you do something in order to be released, you've become a part of it, and have lost your importance.

**Man**  This is your logic. The logic of the system.

**3rd Interrogator**  And are we not living in this system?

**Man**  But like everything else this system is changing.

**3rd Interrogator**  Evolving. And that is why we are so firm, so

faithful, and so kind. (*Pause.*) Listen, you wanted to do
something so that people think you care for them. Now. You
either have to choose to die for this cause, or decide to return
to your comfortable life.

**Man**  Die? For what crime?

**3rd Interrogator**  Here, 'crime' is not the question. The
question is caring for the people, becoming a hero. The people
have not asked you 'Care for us' have they? You want to be
important, to be a hero.

**Man**  You'll make me important, by executing me. And you'll
make a hero out of me. Political prisons are not the grave-yards
of the heroes, but the factories manufacturing them.

**3rd Interrogator** (*laughs*)  The system is not a fool. There are
different ways of killing. Do you think that we blindfold your
eyes and put you in front of the firing squad? And then the
birth of a hero? Wrong. Listen to this, 'A drunken man went
swimming in the sea and the waves brought his body back to
the shore. Or a sleepy driver crashed into the back of a lorry
and died.' (*Laughs.*) This is what we call 'fast killing', 'the
physical way'; but there is a more frightening kind of killing,
which is called 'swimming in acid', 'slow killing'. Dying bit by
bit. When you open the newspaper, in the morning, you will
see your picture and a letter from yourself, in which you have
eloquently praised the system. You turn on the radio and you
hear the announcer saying 'Mr. So-and-So' – yourself – has
been granted medals, awards, scholarships and many other
marks of appreciation for his valuable services to the system.

**Man** *gradually gets frightened.*

Or one day, you see there is an article published in your name
totally in praise of the system – or a book. It can be announced
on T.V. that the system has rewarded you. We can create a
bank account with many zeros and announce it. (*Laugh.*) And
what would you do?

**Man**  It's a lie. It can't work. Everyone will know. Everyone. I'll
write a denial.

**3rd Interrogator** (*laughing boisterously*)  How? You will write to
the press? To the radio? To the T.V? Saying it's a lie? So far so
good. But who can publish it? Broadcast it? Only the system!
Us! You can shout as much as you like, but only in your own

house! The system regards individual freedoms only so far as they cannot harm the freedom of others. You can't even publish a statement, because all the printing houses are run and are controlled by our agents. Right? Unless you have your own printing machines, which is impossible because no one is allowed to have one without the system's permission. Clear?

**Man**  There is always a way. There must be a way.

**3rd Interrogator**  What for? If you did find a way then we'd spread the word that 'he is with the system otherwise he would be arrested, he is one of them otherwise he would be killed.'

**Man**  All this for what? I am not a professional politician, or a member of a party, not a freedom-fighter, I am only someone who feels responsible for society and its people. That's all.

**3rd Interrogator**  People? What responsibility do you feel for the people? Who has given you the right to decide for the people? People are either satisfied or not, if they are, you are against them, and if they are not, they will do something for themselves. By deciding for them, you insult the people's intelligence. You are not thinking about people, no, you are not working for them, you professional protesters are like leeches, sucking people's blood to live.

*The phone rings.* **3rd Interrogator** *picks it up.*

Yes. (*Pause.*) I'm coming.

**3rd Interrogator** *puts the receiver down, and goes out quickly. The* **Man** *is stunned and remains in his place. The wounded prisoner moves and coughs.* **Man** *goes to her with caution.*

**Man**  Was it very bad? (*No reply.*) You've got lots of pain?

**Tied Woman**  I know what to do so that they won't be able to let me live.

**Man**  You won't die.

**Tied Woman**  But I want to die. My death will encourage my comrades.

**Man**  Only a living person can encourage his comrades.

**Tied Woman**  I am one of those who encourages the living by dying.

**Man**  But I want to live.

**Tied Woman** Coward.

**Man** I am afraid. I can't stand getting lashed any more. I don't even have a secret not to reveal.

**Tied Woman** Secret? Make one up. Lie. Join a fake group, an imaginary organisation. Invent stories, tell them about those assassinations you've done, those banks you intended to rob, about the arms you were going to receive. Let them get frightened, confused, and suffer, and then when they torture you for the names and meeting-places, laugh. The more they beat, the louder you laugh, your resistance will torture them.

**1st Interrogator** *enters.*

**1st Interrogator** Well, well our Madame Che Guevara is conscious again. We should have a party in his honour. Everyone and everything is here ready – a dancer, a singer, a poet and the whip, instead of wine. (*Laugh.*) Any objection?

*Silence. He goes to* **Man**, *firmly.*

Sing!

**Man** Pardon?

**1st Interrogator** I said sing a song.

**Man** I am not a singer.

**1st Interrogator** You are what I say you are.

*Picks up a leather belt and comes close to* **Man**.

Sing!

**Man** *remains silent. He goes to the* **Tied Woman**, *whips her very hard, the* **Tied Woman** *writhes.*

Will you sing or should I hit her more?

**Tied Woman** Don't sing!

**1st Interrogator** Shut up! (*Hits her hard with the belt.*)

**Man** I can't sing. Believe me.

**1st Interrogator** (*whips the* **Tied Woman**) Neither can I whip anybody, believe me. (*Laugh.*) Sing, or should I make this whip sing, then?

**Tied Woman** Don't sing.

**1st Interrogator** (*hits* **Man**. *To* **Tied Woman**) Shut up! (*Goes to her and hits her too. To* **Man**.) I'll keep hitting her until you finish a song.

**Man** There is nothing left of her to hit.

**1st Interrogator** (*hits the* **Tied Woman**) She has nine lives.

**Man** Hit me.

**1st Interrogator** Are you telling me what to do? You son of a bitch? Sing!

**Man** I won't if you hit her.

**1st Interrogator** (*hits the* **Tied Woman**) You will.

**Man** *is uncertain, then he starts to sing a popular song. The* **Interrogator** *stops whipping the* **Tied Woman**. *The song is not obviously against the State, but the way he sings it, makes the* **Interrogator** *angry.* **Man** *is going to stop but the* **Tied Woman** *joins in. Hearing her voice,* **Man** *carries on. They both sing together.* **Interrogator** *hits both to silence them. He moves angrily between them and whips them. He puts the belt over the* **Man**'s *mouth and pulls.*

**1st Interrogator** So, I'll arrange a performance for you to really enjoy yourself. In front of millions of people. How about that?

**Man** No!

**1st Interrogator** Yes. Some of your poems, written in praise of the state, with a lot of publicity, you will become the man of the moment. (*He picks up the phone and dials.*) Hello, get me the T.V. controller's office, connect him to my office. (*Puts it down.*)

**Man** No, not even at the cost of my life.

**Interrogator** *leaves the room.* **Man** *pulls himself up to the* **Tied Woman**. *Gets up, holds the* **Tied Woman**'s *head in his hands.*

**Man** This is my death. Finished, everything. (*The* **Tied Woman** *is silent.* **Man** *pulls back frightened, shouts.*) She is dead. Dead. (*Silence. He goes back to her, hugs her, crying.*) You reached your life, and I my death.

*Lights fade to blackout.*

## Scene Six

*A visiting room in prison.*

*It is a small bare room, divided in two parts by a huge frame, covered with chicken wire.* **Woman in veil** *is sitting on a stool, a carrier bag in front of her, waiting downstage. A shout can be heard from outside. Silence. The door upstage opens. The* **Man***, blindfold, is being brought in by* **1st Interrogator***. He leaves the* **Man** *by himself.* **Man** *tries to find his way round with his hands in front of him.*

**1st Interrogator** The visiting regulations have been explained to both of you! Whispering is forbidden. Speaking low is forbidden. Signs are forbidden. The louder you talk the better.

**Man** *reaches the chicken wire.* **Woman** *stands up.* **Man** *tries to find* **Woman***'s hands through the net. Their hands touch each other.*

**1st Interrogator** This is not a place for erotic activities.

*They part their hands, astonished, remaining silent.*

(*Shouting.*) Silence is forbidden.

**Woman** Everybody is well. We all hope you'll be out soon.

**Man** They didn't come after you, did they? They haven't done anything to you, have they?

**Woman** Don't worry about anything. (*Cries.*)

**1st Interrogator** Crying is forbidden.

**Woman** There are some things in the bag, I thought you may need.

**Man** Does anyone think of me out there?

**Woman** Everybody.

**Man** The people?

**Woman** Me.

**1st Interrogator** I don't hear anything.

**Man** They didn't come after you? They haven't done anything to you have they? Have they?

**Woman** (*crying*) They won't come after me.

**Man** You take good care of yourself. You're all I've got left.

**Woman** (*gently*) No!

**Man** Yes.

**Woman** (*low*) No!

**1st Interrogator** Louder.

*Silence*. **Woman** *changes the subject*.

**Woman** They ought to free you, any day now.

**Man** They're putting me on T.V.

**Woman** (*frightened*) No!

**Man** When I think about it, I see that the longer I stay in prison, the more I rot. I can't stand it any longer.

**Woman** What about the people, then?

**Man** They will understand, won't they?

**Woman** Probably!

**1st Interrogator** But it won't change anything for you! Will it?

**Man** Otherwise I stay and rot.

**Woman** You must decide for yourself.

**Man** You think the people want me to die because they need a hero.

**Woman** You always wanted to be a hero.

**Man** My death won't change anything – or will it?

**1st Interrogator** Say YES then.

**Man** How can I look people in the eyes again?

**Woman** Say NO then!

**Man** I don't know what to do.

**Woman** You must decide for yourself. Nobody can help you but yourself.

**Man** What do you all think, my mother, my brothers, my son, you?

**1st Interrogator** They all want you to stay alive. (*To* **Woman**.) Don't they?

**Man** I am alone. I am frightened. And I want to stay alive.

**1st Interrogator** Heroes are only among the dead.

**Man** But if I die . . .?

**Woman** No!

**Man** You will all be sad for a while, then forget – no?

**Woman** We may be proud of you.

**1st Interrogator** Louder.

**Woman** Do whatever you think is best. The decision is yours, just be yourself.

**1st Interrogator** (*shouts*) Silence.

**Man** Would you give me a cigarette?

**1st Interrogator** Visiting time is over.

**Woman** *reaches for her purse, crying.* **1st Interrogator** *takes the* **Man** *towards the door.* **Man** *is resisting.*

**Woman** (*shouting*) No! This visit has cost us a lot. No!

*The lights fade to blackout.*


Scene Seven

*Prison – an open space*

*It is twilight.* **Man** *is tied to a post, ready for execution. An armed* **Guard** *is guarding him. The sound of marching and military commands can be heard from distance. A few lanterns are alight, here and there. The* **Guard** *is rolling a joint.* **Man** *who is pale and sweating from the fear of death, is murmuring something. He is blindfold.*

**Guard** You can talk if you want to. No regulations in the last hour. In the last hour, many sing, many cry, or faint from fear, many shit themselves. Well frankly, it is hard – too hard. It has its own name, 'THE LAST HOUR', but the good thing is that it passes quickly.

**Man** *shouts. The* **Guard** *carries on as though he has heard nothing.*

I have been in the squad for fourteen months, it was really

hard the first weeks. (*Smokes.*) They come to the barracks and shout 'firing squad, one step forward', this means it's voluntary, and there is extra pay as well. But sometimes you can see the boys are frightened, and there are not enough 'volunteers'. Then there is 'selecting' – 'you, you and you', and the firing squad is selected.

**Man** (*shouts*)  I am thirsty.

*The* **Guard** *goes to him. Pours water in his mouth from the canteen.*

**Guard**  Frankly, I pity those sentenced to death. At first when they ordered us to fire I would close my eyes and shoot. But later I realized, the poor convict gets it worse, because when the eyes are shut, the bullet does whatever it wants to do. It hits the thighs, the balls, the hands, the feet, the stomach . . . So now for the prisoner's own sake I shoot right into their heads or their hearts, so they are finished quickly.

**Man**  Butchers.

**Guard**  It works for the squad commanders who have to fire the last shot. Well, they get extra extra pay. It is rumoured that two of them shot themselves in the last fourteen months. And a few got rid of their superiors. Some say they have gone insane.

**Man**  Shut up!

**Guard**  Are you frightened? It is frightening, isn't it? Anyone would be afraid in your place.

**1st, 2nd** *and* **3rd Interrogators** *and some guards enter.*

**3rd Interrogator**  I did my best. But unfortunately, the court verdict is what it was. Death or the T.V.

**Man**  What court? There has never been any court for me!

**1st Interrogator**  The law is the law, whether there is a court or not. What is important is the convict, who is you, and the executioners, who are us!

**Man**  I don't want to die.

**3rd Interrogator**  Who wants to? Death is frightening. Specially for nothing. (*Pause.*) Being alive, in any condition, is better than dying. A person who is paralysed, a man who is blind, or has cancer – a man who is a cripple, or is close to death, has got something that a dead person hasn't got. Life.

**1st Interrogator**  Do you want your eyes open?

**2nd Interrogator**  Don't you want to make your last will?

**Man**  This is savage.

**1st Interrogator**  Or perhaps you want to die while shouting out slogans in praise of the oppressed people?

**2nd Interrogator** (*to the* **guard**)  Close his eyes.

**Man** (*shouts*)  No! I don't want to die.

*The* **Guard** *obeying* **2nd Interrogator***'s order, blindfolds* **Man**. **1st Interrogator** *puts a white cloak on the* **Man**. **3rd Interrogator** *sticks a small red target on him and releases the* **Man** *from the post.* **Man** *not seeing anything, is frightened and comes forward, shivering. The rest aim their guns towards him upstage.*

**Man**  The world will protest against this bestiality.

**3rd Interrogator**  The world, itself, is turning on an orbit of bestiality.

**Man**  My blood will take my revenge. I am innocent.

**3rd Interrogator**  Death or T.V.?

**Man**  I am innocent.

**3rd Interrogator**  Firing squad, forward.

**Man**  You don't have the right to condemn me.

**3rd Interrogator**  You are not being condemned, you are being destroyed.

**1st Interrogator**  Firing squad, attention!

**2nd Interrogator**  And this is the end of a life. The end of a dangerous disease. Death or T.V.?

**Man**  You have no right . . .!

**1st Interrogator**  Take aim.

**Man** (*shouts*)  T.V.

**1st Interrogator**  Fire.

*They shoot in the air. They laugh.* **Man** *bent on his knees in the middle of the yard cries out.*

*Lights fade to blackout.*

## Scene Eight

*A television studio.*

**Man** *sits facing the cameras. An* **Interviewer** *stands by his side, waiting to begin the programme.* **1st Interrogator** *is keeping surveillance.*

**Man**  I am shivering.

**Interviewer**  Nerves. I've worked in television for years. I still get nerves.

**Man**  It is so hot.

**Interviewer**  The lights. Concentrate. Prepare yourself. I want a good programme.

**Man**  It is like facing a firing squad.

**Interviewer**  You face a firing squad once. You can die on television many times. Do you want to go over your speech?

**Man**  I feel dizzy. My mouth is dry. I must use the toilet . . .

**Interviewer**  Stay where you are. Just say what you have to say. We are on stand-by. (*Pause.*) Come on, come on.

**Voice Over**  Twenty seconds.

**Interviewer**  Right. Remember. (*He is afraid.*) Everything.

*He takes his seat. Introductory music fades in and out.*

**Interviewer**  In the name of God and our leader, we now present a special programme. Tonight I am joined in the studio by a brother whose work has been the subject of much discussion. (*To* **Man**.) Good evening, welcome to the programme. (**Man** *nods towards the cameras.*) You are going to talk to me about your political and philosophical beliefs. They have been widely misinterpreted, especially by so-called intellectuals, the poisonous few who seek to corrupt our revolution. As our leader has said – for those against revolution, there awaits the dustbin of death. Now, perhaps, you will begin by saying something about your past?

**Man**  I am . . . I was . . . (*Pause.*)

**Interviewer**  Yes . . .

**Man**  Some of you will know my name. Some of you may have read my work. I am a poet. I (*Pause.*) I have been brought here – I have been invited here, to answer some questions. To give my opinion on matters of interest.

**Interviewer**  Yes. What many viewers would like to know is your attitude to our mighty revolution.

**Man**  Our revolution was made by the people. The people rose against tyranny, greed and hunger. They wanted freedom, homes, meat, equality, onions . . .

**Interviewer**  All of which, thank God, under the leadership of our leader, they now have. Our people today are the most fortunate in the world. Free from idolatrous rule, free to live in comfort. Don't you agree?

**Man**  Cigarette.

**Interviewer**  What?

**Man**  May I have a cigarette?

**Interviewer**  Of course.

**Man**  I don't have any.

**Interviewer**  Here. You were about to say . . .

**Man**  Yes.

**Interviewer**  Yes?

**Man**  Yes.

**Interviewer**  Yes, (*To the cameras.*) he agrees that our country is the only country in the world where our leader's leadership and our Holy law have secured freedom and equality for the people. Good. Let us move on – we would like to hear your views on counter-revolutionary groups, those hypocritical traitors who support the imperialists and wage war on us.

**Man**  I have no direct experience of such groups.

**Interviewer**  (*pause*) Please. Be more precise. What do you mean by direct experience?

**Man**  I am not a member of any group.

**Interviewer**  But what is your opinion of them?

**Man**  I have no personal views. I have not been involved. My views are the same as other people's . . .

**Interviewer** What other people?

**Man** The people who don't belong to a particular party, organisation or group.

**Interviewer** Such people detest fifth columnists, the corrupt puppets of foreign governments.

**Man** So do I.

**Interviewer** What, then is your opinion of our ideology? Do you believe it is the true ideology of the oppressed? (**Man** *doesn't reply.*) Let me repeat the question. Is our belief superior to all other beliefs?

**Man** Matches.

**Interviewer** (*astonished*) What?

**Man** *shows him his cigarette.* **Interviewer** *hands him some matches.* **Man** *lights his cigarette.*

Well?

**Man** In my view. (*Pause. Smokes.*) To be honest I don't know enough about religion or all the ideologies to answer you. I am the son of a poor civil servant. (*Pause.*) I am happy to be here, to have the chance to speak to the people. It is the ambition of every intellectual and artist. But now that I have the opportunity within my grasp I find I've forgotten everything. All I can say is that I am sorry I am . . . I'm sorry that I am . . . thirsty . . .

**Interviewer** Are those foolish people who thought you were a communist mistaken?

**Man** Water . . .

**Interviewer** Are you convinced that our leader is the only true liberator in the world and history?

**Man** *is silent.* **1st Interrogator** *takes out his gun.*

**Interviewer** Are you convinced?

**Man** Yes.

*Lights fade to blackout.*

Scene Nine

*The sitting room.*

**Woman**, *who is showing the first sign of pregnancy, reads a newspaper.* **Man** *watching the flames of a fire outside, from the doorway, drinks from a bottle. There is an exercise bike in the room.*

**Man** Federico Garcia Lorca, was burnt in the fire, the same as Shakespeare. (*Pause.*) Rimbaud as well as Ernesto Che Guevara. From the heart of Omar Khayam, the flames rose alike to those from Bertolt Brecht. Sartre burnt and Trotsky burnt, Lenin burnt and Latin America's poem burnt, Black poems of the struggle burnt, Palestinian poetry burnt, and I burnt. And the lot burnt. (*Laughs.*) Until there weren't any more books left. (*Pause.*) Seventeen years of books. Seventeen years of me collecting books, one by one. All burnt in just a few minutes.

**Woman** Do you think that burning the books is going to make everything alright?

**Man** It makes it change. (*Drinks.*) Haven't you hidden any books or pictures?

**Woman** Not anything good for burning. No!

*Silence.* **Man** *drinks.* **Woman** *reads.*

**Man** Haven't you got fat?

**Woman** This is not fat.

**Man** Yes. It is wind. All the people are blown up. Some from happiness, some from hopelessness. But they all burst the same. (*Pause.*) Machiavelli was blown up in my fire too. He was blown up, blown up and burst. And, together with Marx, turned into ash.

**Woman** Is the torture still going on? Self burning, book burning?

**Man** Still?

**Woman** Your body is still bruised. Your wounds aren't healed yet.

**Man** These are the wounds of the fight. Not torture. Nearly the same, all the drunken fights . . .

**Woman** That night, all the time, my attention was focused on you.

**Man** Thank you. All the time I was getting smashed under the kicks and punches of those drunken bullies, in that deserted road, the lady had been focusing her attention on me. For fuck's sake!! . . .

**Woman** If in prison, they were torturing you, now you're torturing yourself, here.

**Man** What torture? Which prison? All that and my own life were just a test, which I failed.

**Woman** Don't start again. (*Pause.*) You were against them. They arrested you, tortured you. And you denounced yourself, under force, to stay alive and carry on your struggle. That . . .

**Man** You were not there to see how people's youth and lives were ruined in prison; how they could stand those endless tortures and not compromise.

**Woman** You are different.

**Man** It was for your sake that . . .

**Woman** What was for my sake?

**Man** What time is it?

**Woman** What did you want to say about my sake?

**Man** It is getting late.

**Woman** What is it? You are not brave enough even to talk to your own wife?

**Man** Brave? (*Pause.*) My own wife? (*Pause.*) Maybe if I hadn't a wife and kid . . .

**Woman** Blame us. If you think you will be relieved, if you need an excuse . . . I am ready . . .

**Man** All the time, all my fear was that if they came to you or brought you in there.

**Woman** So what? There are so many women rotting in there . . .

**Man** So what? The least danger was rape.

**Woman** (*touching her stomach involuntarily*) The past is past, dead.

**Man** *goes to the bike. Starts to exercise. Long silence.*

**Man**  The body must learn how to resist. The brain must learn how to control the body.

**Woman**  Mum hasn't brought the kid back yet.

**Man**  Come here.

**Woman**  What time is it?

**Man**  Come here! Here!

**Woman** *is not interested. He goes towards her. Stands her up.*

**Man**  Now clench your fist.

*She does so.*

Hold it back and punch me, hard.

*She is uncertain.*

Hurry up. Don't worry, it won't hurt me.

*He holds her hand and forces her to punch him hard in the stomach, for a few punches, then* **Woman** *punches him herself.*

One more. Another one. Harder.

*She stops. Her hand hurts.*

More, please.

**Woman**  I can't, my hand hurts.

**Man**  That was nothing.

*They are standing face to face.*

You must withstand much harder blows from the instruments of torture. (*Turns back.*) I wish . . . I could return to the beginning. (*He cries.*) Do you think there is any way in the whole world for me to make amends? I wish I hadn't been so scared. I wish I hadn't been so frightened, so soon.

**Woman** (*hugs him*)  Do you know how long it is since we made love?

**Man**  What?

*Silence.*

**Woman**  Since you got released.

**Man**   Since I got arrested.

**Woman**   It is a long time. Isn't it?

**Man**   What time is it?

**Woman**   I want to make love.

**Man**   Now?

**Woman**   Now!

**Man**   (*drinks*)   I can't.

**Woman**   Why?

**Man**   I don't know.

**Woman**   Love can cure lots of pains, can't it?

**Man**   Love?

**Woman**   Or have they killed even the love in you?

**Man**   In this pain and despair, this rage and these suspicions, during these sleepless nights and fears and shame, where is the place for love?

**Woman**   Wherever those are. Wherever Man is.

**Man**   Where I am, there is fear of the phone ringing. There is fear of the door bell. There is fear of the sound of car brakes in front of my house. And there is fear of each sound and each motion. There is fear of every stranger and there is fear of every acquaintance and . . . And why does it not rain? I feel so tense.

**Woman**   It's because you drink too much.

**Man**   I want to shout out.

**Woman**   Do then.

**Man**   In there 'being alive' was my painkiller, and out here not being dead is my pain.

**Woman**   Let's go out. You will have some fresh air. Let's go.

**Man**   Out? Outside is full of fear and loneliness. People are so scared of me. My defeat has made me frightening. I'm scared of them too . . . Their mercilessness, their viciousness has made them frightening. Outside, together with me, will be a place full of scared, merciless and lonely victims. Outside, if you go, you'll be the focus of judgement. How easily they judge me! (*Pause.*) Is your hand OK?

**Woman** It will be.

**Man** One good thing about the body is its ability to forget pain, but the spirit . . . Do you want to use something this time?

**Woman** What for?

**Man** To hit me with.

**Woman** Drunk again?

**Man** I am serious.

**Woman** So what?

**Man** I don't know.

**Woman** I know!

**Man** Oh yeah?

**Woman** Leave me alone. I don't have the patience.

**Man** This is not a matter of patience. It's a matter of bravery. A matter of courage. And self confidence. That *you* haven't got. That *you* never had. Had you? Bloody conservative. Remember? No political activities! You always wanted to make an ordinary man out of me. A bloody ordinary satisfied man. A desk-and-office man. A silent, obedient puppet. You wanted me to become like you. But I didn't. Did I? Am I?

**Woman** (*reading the paper*) They've arrested another group.

**Man** (*horrified*) Who are they?

**Woman** Doesn't say.

**Man** Were they armed?

**Woman** Doesn't say!

**Man** (*shouts*) Just what does that stinking paper say?

**Woman** It says that they have arrested yet another group.

*He storms angrily towards her and snatches the paper from her hands.*

**Man** Don't treat me like an idiot.

*He glances greedily at the paper. Pause. He calms down.*

**Woman** Well. What does it say?

**Man** Don't mess with me. I'm nervous.

**Woman** Nervous? You're drunk.

**Man** (*drinks*) Leave me alone.

**Woman** (*drinks*) Why me? (*Pause.*) You're thinking of a man, a man who from the moment you say 'YES' to him, till the end of your days is supposed to stay with you. You are thinking of a room which made you feel giddy with its intoxicating freshness, its silence, and strangeness from the moment it was filled with tiredness and hope by the noise of kids. Kids who are yours. You are thinking of a bed that from the naked moment of joy to the cloistered moment of the coffin, is supposed to be the place of ravishing whispers of love. And you are thinking of all the millions of girls all over the world who are waiting for what you have already achieved. And you think. And you think. (*Drinks. Goes towards the bottle, fills the glass.*) If I wasn't happy to participate in those suspicious meetings, if I wasn't happy that you participated in those suspicious meetings, it was because of my fear. I was scared to lose what I had. What we had. I was scared because I didn't understand what you were talking about. Because you didn't know what you were all talking about. Because I saw you scared. I saw you in doubt. And I saw you wasted. (*Pause.*) Intellectual debates in safe shelters, under the shadow of satisfying fears and heroism.

**Man** We just wanted to do something for the people.

**Woman** Which kind of people? Those whose language, culture and dress, is different. Those whose disease and whose smell of sweat and even whose death is different to the lot of you? Those people who don't know you, who look daggers at you not understanding your language? Or those people who do speak your language, do dress like you and build the jails?

**Man** (*angrily*) Shut up. You have no right to talk like this to someone who has gone to jail, has been tortured, has been insulted and . . . and has destroyed himself and all for the people.

**Woman** If my silence would solve anything then I'd shut up. But it doesn't. One who does go to jail, does get tortured, and all for the people, is not destructible. Not believing in the people is what destroys. That causes one to deviate and that is why today you are taking out your defeat on me, yourself, and the people. (*Pause. Drinks.*) That night in that street, it was you who tempted those drunken bullies and don't deny it. I was carefully watching you all the time.

**Man**   That is enough.

**Woman**   But I want to talk. (*Pause.*) You yourself tempting them to rape me. (*Laughs bitterly.*) And if they hadn't been too drunk . . .!

**Man**   You think that I couldn't handle those bullies? I only wanted to test your resistance.

**Woman** (*imitates the* **Man**)   Lift your skirt up, higher, higher. (*She laughs.*) Have you got the guts to touch her? Look, do you want her to take her blouse off?

**Man** (*shouts*)   I just wanted to test you.

**Woman** (*imitating*)   I withstand the most cruel and deadly tortures, I spit at you and I shout NO! And if you cowardly butchers feel weak and doubtful, you'd better get lost and go back to your hideout empty handed. (*Shouts.*) Test?!!

**Man** (*bitter*)   If there is faith, if the moral is high, then you can withstand, resist.

**Woman**   And for a slight weakness, a few shortcomings, turn the struggle into a personal, petty, masochistic debate.

**Man**   It seemed to me very simple. Like a game. I only wanted to test you. (*Pause.*) All the time in jail I was afraid that they would come after you. I thought if they were to bring you there, and if in front of me . . .? That night I also wanted . . .

**Woman** (*interrupts*)   Come after me? Take me there? In front of you? (*Explodes.*) What is the difference here or there? In front of you or in your absence? Evin is everywhere. Evin is here.

**Man** (*nervous*)   This is a foolish comparison. Where were you when the door opened and the torturer entered with that thick, black, wire cable to explain Evin to those bodies congealed with blood and infected wounds? (*Pause.*) Without a wife, maybe I wouldn't have shown weakness.

**Woman**   Your weakness is not at all related to your having a wife. I am not saying that you were not worried about me, but I can say that you were not worried about me for my sake. (*Laughs.*) What am I saying? It looks as if I'm drunk too!

**Man**  For whose sake was it that I was content to give up my pride and future and, and everything else so that my wife wouldn't . . . ?

**Woman**  (*interrupts*) That's just the problem. Me or 'your wife'? You'd only find my being raped unacceptable – you know why? – because a possession of yours has been used.

**Man**  It hasn't happened because my weakness made you safe.

**Woman**  (*laughs aloud*) Safe? You said yourself, you were worried that something would happen in front of you. Which it didn't. For you the arena of torture, rape, cruelty and struggle is still in the jail, and only the jail in which you're captive. Is not that so? (*No reply.*) Isn't it? You alone are not the whole world and that which happens in front of your eyes is not all that happens the whole world over.

**Man**  Even you're humiliating me, taunting me.

**Woman**  I am talking to you, truthfully and with love, because I know that you are full of love for the masses. But I feel that you are on the brink of a collapse into the abyss that your torturers and interrogators are pushing you towards. The abyss of despair, masochism and isolation. And if you are not aware . . .

**Man**  Awareness?

**Woman**  Don't interrupt me. Your life is out there. Among the people, and not in here and in yourself. And remember that neither I nor anyone else is to blame for anyone's weakness.

**Man**  (*explodes*) How very brave. How revengeful. How revolutionary. Sitting at home and judging is so easy. You haven't been their captive, their plaything. You haven't tasted the real meaning of jail, torture and the interrogator.

**Woman**  Let's not have a competition between ourselves or the people about our experiences of torture.

**Man**  (*shouts*) What competition when you don't know anything about them?

**Woman**  This is my torture! (*Lifts up her blouse.*) I feel it with my blood, womb and anger. And I will feel it in the future.

*Lights fade to blackout.*

## Scene Ten

*The morgue.*

*The scene is set in a mortuary. The place is very unlike its kind in the Christian tradition. This is generally a room where, according to Muslim tradition, a mortician, or 'washer of the dead' cleans and prepares the dead prior to burial. Using a basin of water, he then wraps the bodies up in a white muslin sheet and puts them on stone platforms. The dead are then carried out and placed in graves – a mound of corpses. A huge pile of clothes. The mortician is washing a corpse in the water basin. A hunch-backed youth comes in at intervals and carries the dead out.* **Man** *is drunk, sitting on an empty coffin.*

**Mortician** (*to the corpse he is washing*) Loosen up. Don't go rigid on me. This is the last fling . . . Agile, you must have been, billy-goat like, if I'm not mistaken . . . surely you have seen twenty summers, hapless creature. What did you get horny for? Which demon giant was to be slain . . .? It's not a wound this, it's a gaping cave . . . But it doesn't seem you have lived unfulfilled, you gad-about. (*Turns to* **Man**.) How about some of that white-satan of yours?

**Man** *bring a pocket-flask out and hands it to him. The hunch-backed* **Youth** *comes in and takes a body out.* **Mortician** *drinks.*

When I see a corpse, as I go over him, before my thumb touches his head, I like to know all about him – actions, words 'n' all. (*Drinks.*) The tongue would have been of no use otherwise, if not for such talks and expressions . . . I wouldn't have lasted without these expressions. Am I chin-wagging?

**Man** I wasn't listening.

**Mortician** Good! (*To the* **Youth** *who is carrying a body out.*) We're nearly done.

**Man** What time is it?

**Mortician** Almost daybreak.

**Man** *stretches out and takes the flask from* **Mortician** *and drinks a few mouthfuls.*

What do you see in this caboodle? I haven't figured you out yet. You don't let on. Silent as the grave, like a corpse – may you never be one. (*Takes the flask.*) To be honest, the first few nights my intuition said that you were a cop, an agent or something. Now I suspect your case is to do with love, a kind of affair of the heart. Isn't it? (*No reply*.) Have they done in your beloved?

**Man**  Who?

**Mortician**  The one you're looking for.

**Man**  I am looking for my own corpse. I am trying to get even with me.

**Mortician**  (*does not grasp his meaning*)  What's the use of spending your time in this stinking, God-forsaken dump? You couldn't even bribe a hyena to stay here.

**Man**  I want to find out what I've escaped from. I want to see how I would have looked, if I'd said 'NO'. I seek to find myself. Besides, where else can I hide away from the humiliation, from whisperings?

**Mortician**  What are you? A spy? NO! I don't reckon you're one of these.

**Man**  Haven't you seen me on television?

**Mortician**  (*laughs*)  Television? These ever changing corpses, wounded, blown up, shredded to pieces, the young and the aged, children with skins which resembles rose petals are my television. Huh, television! Are you an actor?

**Man**  A repentant.

**Mortician**  *takes the flask and drinks. Gets up and begins to check the pockets in the clothes pile. The* **Youth** *is back.*

**Mortician**  (*to* **Youth**)  It's time. Go and get your teeth into some grub, hit the sack, off with you, orphan.

**Youth**  *exits.*

**Man**  Just to stay alive.

**Mortician**  (*pointing to a corpse*)  This one resists my intuition. But he looks as if he lived worrying for others. He must have had a lot of worries. He is not out of his forties yet look at him, look at his hair! Snow-drifts over a grave.

**Man**  Why change the subject? Spit and say what a wanker I am, that I shouldn't have bitten off more shit than I could chew.

**Mortician** Come off it. What else can I say? I don't want to rub more salt in your wounds. If you were forced to, well, everyone will get the picture. They all know a put-up job when they see one!

**Man** If they know, why do they turn their heads and spit as I go by?

**Mortician** (*sits next to* **Man** *and drinks*) They all know the score. You're not the first one and won't be the last. Those who turn their heads and give you dirty looks, if right, should roll their sleeves up and show the flag. Show their balls.

**Man** Fear. I sold out because of fear. Fear of death . . . I am so impure that all the spitting in this world cannot cleanse me and . . .

**Mortician** Let's say you're on the level, so what the hell are you doing here?

**Man** I told you. The tranquillity of death. Security. I am looking for my own corpse.

**Mortician** Nah! You shy away from your own corpse. When you see these mute bodies your knees perk up, your heart finds vigour. Why? Because you realize you still exist and you still honour the world with your presence. You think people go to the cemetery to weep? Wrong! They have the same tale as yours; their bloody intuition gets satisfied. Because others lie under and they don't. They're on the top, fat and fortified.

**Man** Will you wash me?

**Mortician** For someone in my position all corpses are the same. Good or bad, pretty or not, when you get here you're a dumb stiff.

**Man** I said will you wash me now?

**Mortician** Have you gone off your rocker? One over the eight are we?

**Man** (*takes a handful of money out and offers it to* **Mortician**) In the same basin. Right next to this one in here.

**Mortician** Lie down. Look dead. Behave like a corpse. It's useless. Suppose I wash your body, what the hell will you do with your mind?

*Takes the money.* **Man** *stands up and begins to undress. There is a commotion outside. Suddenly a young* **Fugitive** *stumbles in.* **Man** *and* **Mortician** *are dumb-founded.*

**Fugitive**　Any other exits here?

**Mortician**　This is the last exit.

**Fugitive**　How can one escape from here?

**Mortician**　Why does one come here at all?

**Fugitive**　They're after me.

**Man**　What have you done?

**Fugitive**　I was found out.

**Man**　You think I can help?

**Fugitive**　I was trapped. My comrades don't know.

**Man**　Pretend you are dead. Lie down among the corpses.

**Mortician**　Are you kidding? Where there's a soul, it shines a mile off.

**Fugitive**　They think if they capture me, they'll get the whole lot of us. Bloody executioners!

*The* **Fugitive** *looks outside through a crack in the door.*

The whole place is surrounded! (*Turns to them.*) One of you must do me a favour.

**Man**　What?

**Fugitive**　(*takes a piece of paper out*) Call this number. Deduct a 2 from each figure. Tell them 'THE SKY IS CLOUDY, THE BIRD HAD TO FLY'. Memorize it.

**Man**　The sky is cloudy, the bird had to fly . . . Well?

**Fugitive**　(*looks disturbed and paces around*) Do you have a crowbar or a walking stick?

**Mortician**　(*picks up a stick and hands it to the* **Fugitive**) Here. I use it to ward off rabid cats and dogs. The smell of blood brings 'em here.

*There is a commotion. A whistle is blown.* **Fugitive** *hurriedly hides the stick under her garment.* **Man** *looks hesitant and tried to hide. Two*

**Agents** *accompanied by armed guards enter. They quickly take up positions in the corners of the room.*

**1st Agent** Nobody move!

**2nd Agent** The place is surrounded.

**1st Agent** (*to* **Mortician**) You! Move aside. Remove your bloody carcass. (**Mortician** *obeys. To* **Fugitive**.) Now, you stay put. I'll make chicken wire out of you if you put one foot wrong. You parasite.

**Fugitive** You are the parasites! Executioners.

**2nd Agent** OK talkative bitch. Come on sing. We'll sort you out in Evin.

**Fugitive** All dogs behave like lions at their master's gate.

**1st Agent** We'll get even.

**2nd Agent** You are going to sing like a nightingale and your friends'll be there, listening to you.

**Fugitive** We'll see. Executioner!

**1st Agent** Now turn around. Gently! One false move and I'll blow your fucking head off! Is that clear?

**Fugitive** I am not going to Evin! (*Raises her hands. Looks at* **Man** *and* **Mortician**.) My heart is a red star on the flag of the people.

*She takes the stick out. Points it like a gun at them. The guards go on their stomachs and fire. The* **Fugitive** *falls. The guards examine her with caution.*

**1st Agent** She's dead. Whore!

**2nd Agent** (*to* **Mortician**) You haven't seen anything.

**Mortician** As you say.

**2nd Agent** Shut up.

**Mortician** As you wish.

**1st Agent** (*as he empties the pockets of the* **Fugitive**) Don't let them wash this bitch!

**2nd Agent** (*gazing at* **Man**) Who's this?

**1st Agent** (*approaches* **Man**. *Looks at him and bursts out laughing.*) He's quite well known! He's one of us. (*To* **Man**.) How the hell are you, brother? (*Examines the flask, smells it smiling.*)

**2nd Agent**  You know him?

**1st Agent**  Sure! He is a repentant. A famous one at that!

*Gives the flask to* **Man**.

**2nd Agent** (*to the guards*)  That's all.

**1st** *and* **2nd Agents** *exit.* **Man** *is dishevelled.* **Man** *looks angry and tearful. Outside a whistle is blown. Hurried footsteps. He bends over the* **Fugitive**, *lifts the stick and squeezes it in his palm and turns to* **Mortician**.

**Man** (*crying aloud*)  Wash this tormented soul! Wash us!

*Lights fade to blackout.*


Scene Eleven

*A graveyard*

*Photographs of the young martyrs stand by each grave. A spring pumps blood in the middle of stage. The* **Contact** *is standing in front of the audience. A group of mourners are singing a mourning song over a grave.* **Man**, *sitting by a new grave, is watching them.*

**Contact**  A man has run using the code words. I was appointed to make contact with him. But we shouldn't be careless! We watched him for some time, then we made different appointments in different places, till at last, today, after changing a few cars, he is here! It doesn't seem to us that he's a bait to lead us into a trap, although we are well prepared! But the strange thing is that he has a very naive request! He's asking for something which isn't within my authority to refuse or accept. Although the answer, from the higher committee to these sort of things, is usually obvious! Besides, we haven't had a case like this before, where a man comes and says; I want to join the organisation. That simple! And we say 'yes' or 'no'. That simple! (*Pause.*) Usually a freedom fighter who wants to join the organisation must be either recommended or introduced by two full members! This one says I want to join! He expects me to say 'yes' or 'no'. Simple as that. But it isn't that simple. There are other unusual factors to consider. (*Turns to* **Man**.) The unusual factor here, my friend, is you! Look! As you say yourself, you're a famous person, and this fame makes your case even more complicated. No doubt you were a progressive man, but you were forced to appear on telly to admit you were wrong! You expressed your disgust and regret. This makes your case more difficult for us!

**Man**  I am not the only one who was made to express his regret!

**Contact**  That is right. But you did it on telly, didn't you?

**Man**  On television or in the papers or behind closed doors, what difference does it make?

**Contact**  I accept almost everything you have just said. But one who shows his weakness, please don't take it personally, has sat the exam and . . .

**Man**  (*interrupts*)  Is not trustworthy!

**Contact**  Not completely. There've been cases where some comrades, after denouncing their beliefs, have turned to the struggle and then becomes martyrs. But in your case . . .

**Man**  What about my case?

**Contact**  Your fame!

**Man**  Look! I haven't had party training. I am not a man with experience of guerrilla war. But I suppose if I had had this kind of training and experience, the case now would be entirely different.

**Contact**  Listen. They both know you! The people and the system! And this makes you scared. That is why you want to join . . .

**Man**  Joining a political organisation means I'm scared?

**Contact**  Some people do heroic things when they're scared!

**Man**  Even so, there is nothing wrong with it. Fear has created a lot of heroes! And who knows if your own reason for joining the party wasn't your fear? Fear isn't anything less than love.

**Contact**  I'm just trying to explain . . .

**Man**  All the people know that I was forced, like many others, don't they?

**Contact**  So does the prisoner himself. And that's why this matter should be looked at from another angle as well. Look! You as a prisoner know that people are aware of the pressure put upon you when you make a confession and denounce yourself. So you could do it completely willingly and in obedience to the system. Even at your own suggestion.

**Man** (*stunned*) That's ridiculous.

**Contact** It's intelligent. You'll be freed. The system will be happy defeating you.

**Man** The system can make you express your regret secretly, and free you as a hero, if there is a deal between you and them.

**Contact** It can. But this kind of freedom is a silent one. The system gets nothing because the majority of people know you as a political prisoner when you are free, accompanied by a lot of propaganda. All the benefit's for the prisoner who's compromised himself for the system.

**Man** Where in the world is there anything to benefit a political prisoner?

**Contact** It's very simple! When the system says; 'Look people, I freed this political prisoner because I am kind even to those who oppose me,' people will say; 'Look . . . they arrested him. They tortured him and then made him denounce himself under force. But they can't fool us. He is our hero, because he struggled for us.' (*Pause.*) But the prisoner . . . who is compromised, remains as the winner.

**Man** (*angrily*) Listen, I was tortured and forced to go on television and recant my entire life's work. In front of millions of eyes, my very being, my soul was raped. Now tell me, where the fuck is the benefit in that for me?

*A whistle. The* **Contact** *goes among the mourners and* **Man** *stays, uncertain. The mourners are ready for any unexpected event. Their guns can be seen. An* **Old Woman***, wearing a black veil, appears crying silently. She is in search of a particular grave.*

**Old Woman** (*to* **Contact**) Have they buried the new ones here? The ones who got killed this week? (*No reply.*) Where've they buried our dead?

**Contact** In the new part, mother. At the end of the graveyard!

**Old Woman** Thanks! I am looking for the grave of my fourth one. Thanks a lot.

*She goes out. A whistle.* **Contact** *goes back to* **Man**.

**Contact** I do understand your situation and your feelings.

**Man** You don't understand because you weren't there. Because you were not me in there! You can't judge the taste of acid from its formula. You . . . all of you . . . the free people of the Earth, can't judge the loneliness, fear, the need to stay alive, as a political prisoner can. At this very moment thousands of prisoners, girls and boys, are being raped and we are turning our eyes away. Wasting our time making judgements.

**Contact** All of us, everywhere in the world, are being raped. Even outside prisons. And this gives us the right to judge.

**Man** Foolish play with words. The rape you are talking about is general, like the word itself. And at this very moment when the whole world of yours is being raped, I am being raped too, as a small part of a total phenomenon. But as a whole body of a single and small world, which is me, and only me, I am being raped twice, inside the prison. I am a doubly raped victim.

**Contact** Everybody, everywhere and anyhow, has the right to judge. Man is his own judgement!

**Man** I am tired. Tired of words and explanations. I want to fight and fighting by yourself, alone, is already a defeat!

**Contact** I, by myself, as I told you before, can't give you a final and clear answer. We'll consider your request. But what is clear and important, is your action and struggle for the future. (*Pause.*) Anyway, I thank you for your help and . . .

**Man** I didn't come here for your thanks. I am here to get a clear-cut answer to my request.

**Contact** Unfortunately there is no clear-cut answer to give you now.

**Man** (*angry*) You and your organisation, like the past that didn't absorb me, are responsible for the waste of my energy and my abilities. And you are going to kill my determination to fight. The submerging of me and the others like me in the quick-sand of the system is nothing but the pollution of your well.

*Lights fade to blackout.*

Scene Twelve

*The sitting room*

**Man** *is on an exercise bike.* **Woman** *is knitting.*

**Woman**  Naked, in front of the mirror it was me staring at my swelling stomach, motionless. Motionless I was and yet I saw myself beating my own stomach, hard, to bleed. Do you know how many times the empty bath turned full of blood, before my hesitant eyes? Do you know how many times, standing by the window, I watched myself crashed, down on the ground beneath, blood all over my deformed body? The blood of my bastard foetus? (*Pause.*) Do you think I didn't have dreams of tearing out my womb? Do you think I didn't have painful and bloodstained nightmares? (*Pause.*) I could have got rid of it to make it nothing in your eyes. But no, my hatred is bigger than that. I want it to grow. I want myself to feel this flourishing rage. You know why? It is and will be mine and not theirs. So it'll see the world as I'll want it to see. I want to feed and to grow my child of savagery, their living nightmare. I'll mother it with love to grow my image of revenge . . .

*The phone rings.* **Woman** *picks up the phone.*

**Woman**  Hello. Hello? (*Pause.*) Hello? (*Puts the phone down. Looks at* **Man**.) What are you thinking about? (*No reply.*) Is it too hard?

**Man**  What?

**Woman**  Enduring me? (*No reply.*) I'm thinking of leaving. I think it may help you. I think when you look at me, you are looking at your wounds. I think our pains and wounds, together, are not endurable, under the same roof. I think our combined cries will bring the roof down on our heads.

**Man** *goes out to the other room.* **Woman** *dries her tears.* **Man** *comes back with a pistol in his hand.* **Woman** *freezes, seeing it.*

**Woman**  What do you want to do?

**Man** (*holds the pistol close to* **Woman**'s *head*)  Have you thought of a place to go where your wounds can't go with you? Where *our* wounds can't come with you? Have you thought that these wounds will be with us, open-mouthed and decayed, *while* there's life and *while* I breathe? Have you thought that the only way to escape is my death?

**Woman** Don't be foolish.

**Man** My death will be the death of our wounds.

*The phone rings. He is stunned. The phone rings. He goes to the phone, picks it up and listens.*

Hello. Yes, that's me . . . Yes I recognized you. Yes . . . When? Certainly. Where? Yes I know where it is. (*Pause.*) Yes I'll be there on time. No, of course. (*Puts the phone down.*) Certainly! It was death! (*Goes back to his bike.*) Death! He said there are some manuscripts. They can't trace the writer by themselves. He said as an expert I must help them. I have to. He said they won't forget my help. He said they will repay me in the future! He said . . .

**Woman** Who?

**Man** My interrogator! Your child's father! Death!

**Woman** Going?

**Man** Don't you want me to go? Death is death!

**Woman** I thought after all these agonies and torture, you were able to distinguish between death and death. I thought you had chosen that pistol to . . .

**Man** To wash away my wounds with my blood? What's the difference between suicide or collaborating with them? Death is death! (*He laughs.*) You want a distinguished death for me! Disintegrated temples on the heart of revenge! (*Low.*) Death is death!

**Woman** And I am going to mourn your living death.

*Lights fade to blackout.*

Scene Thirteen

*The sitting room*

**Woman** *is packing her suitcase. Taking things from here and there. She is by the bike, touching it. The door bell rings. Then the sound of heavy knocking on the door with hands and feet.*

**Woman** I am coming!

*The door breaks down. A few armed men make their way in. They start to search everywhere.* **3rd Interrogator** *comes in.*

**Woman**   What is it? What are you looking for?

**3rd Interrogator**   Shut up, you whore!

*The armed men finish their search. One of them shakes his head when* **3rd Interrogator** *looks at him.*

**3rd Interrogator**   (*to* **Woman**)   Where is he?

**Woman**   Who?

**3rd Interrogator**   Your pimp husband.

**Woman**   He had an appointment with one of you lot.

**3rd Interrogator**   Don't play that game with me. I'll find him even if I have to turn this place inside out, or set fire to the whole city. (*Pause.*) I am going to find him. And I'll make your whore mother mourn for you. Now you talk, before I make you sing. Where is that murderer hidden?

**Woman**   I told you! One of your lot rang him . . .

**3rd Interrogator**   (*beats her*)   You are not dealing with a bunch of blind fools. (*Pointing to the suitcase.*) Where are you running away to? Where are you going to meet him?

**Woman**   Nowhere! I'm going to the North. I have found a job in a small factory. I was heading . . .

**3rd Interrogator**   I'll arrange an unforgettable journey for you to enjoy, every pissing moment of it.

*He signals to the armed men to beat the* **Woman**. *They start doing so.*

Will you talk or do you want me to make you?

**Woman**   What's happened? He came to help you. He came to be at your service. Don't beat me. I am pregnant.

*An armed man holds his rifle up, aiming to hit the* **Woman** *in the stomach. Lights go. Only a spotlight on the* **2nd Interrogator** *downstage.*

**2nd Interrogator**   Usually our organisation makes such an appointment with those who don't seem to endanger us, and our system's security. These kinds of appointments have two advantages. First of all we will reassess their mental and ideological status. Do they want to be connected with us? Are they prepared to co-operate with the system? And secondly, we remind them that they are still being watched, and that they must be constantly careful. Well, where do we meet these people? In a quiet place? No! In a crowded place? No! In a quiet, crowded place? Yes! A quiet place where ordinary people are not to be found. A crowded place full of the relevant intellectuals, involved with the same affairs. Why? Because these ex-prisoners must feel that they are on the spot all the time – and that they are being seen with some suspicious persons who are ourselves, of course. And that is to make them scared and ashamed. And then they will be their own enemy and their own watchdogs. (*Pause.*) This mother-fucker arrived on time. We were watching him from the Toyota, in front of the restaurant. He went in. We saw him looking around. He found his interrogator. He went to him. He sat on the chair next to him. He started to talk. It was only after half an hour that all the people were hurriedly leaving the restaurant. We got out of the car and rushed inside. He had disappeared in the crowd. We lost him. The waiter said: 'When the shooting broke out, all the people made a crowd around him, to help him get away. No one saw when or how he vanished.' He said: 'All the attention was on the man drowning in his own blood.' (*Pause.*) That man was our best interrogator. The martyr of the organisation.

*Lights come on. The armed man hits the* **Woman** *in the stomach. She screams. They leave her for a while. She miscarries. Blood all around her. She stains her face with the blood. A spotlight on* **Woman**.

**Woman**  So that I
Prometheus
the prisoner of time
may believe
how alone I am left,
how defeated I am left.
But I Prometheus. . . .

*Lights fade to blackout.*

# Poems

*For Rob Ritchie*

### The Basket

Where is your body?
Where is your tender body?
The body that never was
a refuge for me
The body that never was
a shelter for me

The fresh flowers of
your body
weren't for the garden
of my hands
The tale of your
flourishing hands
was nothing but
the lamentation
of my defeat

Look
Look, the termites
ate my precious
chest of memories
Look
Look, without the birds of
your voice
the wind took away
the jasmines of my songs

Cowards with the buds of
fractures
I am a tree
in the path of the storm
Look
Look at me
How cold
How wounded and mournful
I stand at the threshold of
Shattering

Your departure
was the fall of my
love's grey star

Your tender name
wasn't the song

It was a dirge
for my arrival

Where is your body?
Where is your tender body?
The body that never was
a refuge for me
The body that never was
a shelter for me

### Evin

**Evin** is as intimate as a sister crying
As domestic as a grandfather's ancient fear
**Evin** is as heartbreaking as a mother's tears
In the hidden weeping nights of the father
As revengeful as brother's blood in the leaden dawns of
executions
**Evin** is as forgotten as I am
As real as we are
On the anniversaries of daggers and hate **Evin** is as venerable
as
Fearful orders of massacres, celebrating the terrified
executioners' longevity
Against the shadows of torture, firing squad, wall and bullet-
squall
**Evin** is as questing as a prisoner's shout for freedom to flourish
**Evin** is as strong as belief and awareness
As high as roaring NO over the grave of rotten YES
**Evin** is as young as the people and I
As old as the fresh-born child of the Earth
**Evin** is as elusive as a star-hunting leopard
**Evin** is as common as Pinochet or Somoza
**Evin** is in the Philippines, in Poland
**Evin** is in South Africa, in Turkey, and in Korea
**Evin** is as cosmopolitan as our sufferings
As our struggle
**Evin** is not just a prison
**Evin** is not only in Iran
**Evin** is not just mine, look around
**Evin** is a gigantic bloated corpse of violated yesterdays on the
wounded shoulders of today.
**Evin** is here
**Evin** is everywhere.

### Woman In Red

My Iran is not a woman of silk
raised to muslin and rivers of milk
a woman of dreams and pampered ease
asleep on a litter of emerald beads
winding through labyrinths of song

My Iran is not a nymph of the fields
a goddess of night, a temptress who yields
a painted beauty, perfumes, composed,
within whose arms love lies enclosed

My Iran is not the talk of the dance
the object of an indolent glance,
the enchanter in the tilted cup
on nights of lute and viol

My Iran is a woman, red with flashing rage,
a virgin in love, an innocent in a cage,
with whose deadly kiss the butcher is repaid
blasted apart by the plague of grenades
she wears on her fresh young breasts.

### Little Karim

You little Karim,
Karim with nightlike eyes,
Karim of silent courage,
what did the stars sing
that night paused to let you pass?
Of which secret did
the gossiping wind speak
to the wounded mountain-bay
and the moonshine spread the pattern
of your presence on which spring
that the ruined village
came to welcome you

You little Karim
Little Karim of blasted Sannandaj[1]
Karim of secret wanderings
tell me how you
hung your heart
like a lantern in the doorways
of the destitute, in the villages

of poverty?
How you brought your youth
from newly destroyed houses to old huts?

How did you divide love among the empty
napkins
how did you define freedom
among the harassed gatherings
on the farewell kisses' bridge:
bread, arms and youth
from the huts of captivity
to the fronts of liberty.
And this long queue of trust
lovingly parades ahead
from night ambush to dawn back at base.

You Karims of labour and equality
Karims of the equal future
Karims of Peshmargeh[2]
What did you sing in the wind?
What did you write on the stones?
What did you say to the soil?
That seasonal workers pack their bundles toward you
and wheat growers open their arms of harvests for you.

You victorious Karims of tomorrow
you great Karims
Karims of Kurdistan
the sun will pause for you to pass.

[1] *Name of a city in Kurdistan.*
[2] *Kurdish freedom fighters*


### Drifting On A Strange Soil

Drifting on a strange soil
drifting endlessly.
Where is my birthplace
fellow wanderer?

In the drifting nights of anxiety
when I want to cry out for the world
in which language shall I call you?
In which accent shall I sing for you?

I am
in this city that has given me a refuge
bitter, lost, and pastless.
All the alleys lead to strangeness
which direction would bring us together?

Drifting on a strange soil
drifting endlessly.
Where is my birthplace
fellow wanderer?

In which alley
did the first greetings
fill me with ballads?
In which square
did the last farewell
sadden my love songs?

Houses,
alleys,
streets
blank diaries.
You and I
the pastless aged
seasons,
memoryless passing seasons.

Drifting on a strange soil
drifting endlessly.
Where is my birthplace
fellow wanderer?

Build me a shelter
from memories
the sand-wind
brakes the rootless willow
strange soil
forgets the pastless old plough

I want to fill my hamper of memories
from the green flowerbed of today
I want to fill the city of my oldness
by the perfume of becoming a flower again

Drifting on a strange soil
drifting endlessly.
Where is my birthplace
my fellow wanderer?

### Chic-a Chic-a Chic Chich

O you children of the famine
bring your dreams, your colourful
dreams of a piece of bread
and another piece
fragrant dreams of meat in the pan
fresh dreams of dewdrops from
spearmint and radish
O you children of stagnation
bring your dreams

The train passes through the wind
Chic-a chic-a chic chich . . .

O you girls of givings and takings
bring your love, your forbidden love
your imprisoned love from the closet of declines
bring your love for refreshing the world
from beneath the barren garden beds
your love for renewing the sun
from the bundles of creases
your love of giving birth to the future
from the forgotten shelves
O you ruined girls
bring your loves
the train is passing through the mist
Chic-a chic-a chic chich . . .

O you women for sale
O you men for rent
bring your tears, the tears dropped
on the paints and oils of your labour
bring your anger, the anger broken on the
strings and trellis of captivity
bring your desire, crushed between
the jaws of barter
bring your youth, burnt in the mouth
of deceitful kilns
O you women of tolerance

O you men of bitterness
bring your rage, your dagger
we are heading for the stations of
the waiting revolutions.

The train passes through the storm
Chic-a chic-a chic chich . . .

### Night Sun

Tortured me
to justify
the ruling night.
Beat me hard
to write just
love songs.
Although
he's lashed me again
again I have to make whips
with my poems.

He is making a night-tale
for you to stay asleep

To shake you awake
I must make a song
of my blood

I am able to make a green
shelter
from my song
for you the tired
to rest

I am able
to let flow a flood
from my roaring
river of songs
upon this thirsty soil

To defeat this savage night
from the dawn of my blood
I am able to make
the sun rise
nightly.

This flower-killing season
comes each winter
I am able to grow blooms
from the season of my heart
for thousands of springless gardens

In the leaden dawn of
execution
I am able to make my breasts
a refuge
for the red flowers of
our love.

You are able
to sing a song
in the revolutions
I am able to make new songs
in victory

### Mother, Me And The New Year

Apple, greenery, coin
by the mirror
the hasty goldfish of the pond
in the limpidity of a thin jar
the new red-ribboned frame
and the last picture of my father.
Like the spreaded jasmine perfume
an ambiguous delight
treads into the house
by the window,
mother peeps out into the alley
the long locked window
opens
perfume, light and noise
grows
a passerby's song shrinks away:
'it's flower
it's spring'
peering through a book
at mother
she isn't in black
I relish
she raptures.

By the storm of joy
the wrinkles on her face
turn red
turn white
I smile
she smiles
and it's new year.

## Shelter Song

Blood in the streets
rage indoors
young girls buried
in ancient graves
love is a bullet
in the handsomest breast

Fear sings from every roof
songs shelter down deep wells
lips are sealed
walls shout
in nightly raids
paint obliterates
each new slogan
and death celebrates

I must think up the most gracious name
for her who falls to the dust, red
from that very last bullet
and think of a most loving rage

Rain at dawn
hatred in the shelters
whose grave shall I cry over?
Which corpse shall I mourn for?
Farewell little lark
farewell my daughter!

## The Flood of Sunrise

When you kill a lantern
it becomes moonshine.
When you break a star
the sun rises.

When you clinch the neck of
this rose
One spring flower blooms
out of its sap

You can't lash silence
this roaring sea
mountain-waves rising
from each water-drop.

Fright-shivering anxiety
pales the face of
the executioner
from the comrade's rage-laughter

In the rainless garden
this is the rose's shout
which stamps lightnings
on the sterile sky

In the heated womb of
this motionless night
what a floodlike pure sunrise
is flourishing

Rain my blood
over this naked land
on which a red forest of passion
will grow

Cry-like red hands
unfold to the sun
streets of
waving flags

There it is
the red garment of
the comrades over the
shoulders of the city

Look
to what stature revolution
is rising.
Look!

### Farewell

Farewell
Ballads,
Setaar[1],
and stars
wine,
roses
and lanterns
and a roof
which knows your songs.

Teach my rifle
a flower-like ballad of love.

[1] *An Iranian instrument.*

### From The Last Moment

How red the rain of your hair flies back
from my burst breast
while the heat of my beating temples
gives the burnt petals of your kiss to the wind
explosions sing through the window with the night
cold

Bitter butterflies fly from the stars of your eyes
and love cries
the high wings of dawn stretch from the wounded
shoulders of the comrades
oh where is that red scarf?

### Love Me My Love

In this strangeness
with its cold days and nights,
Stranger to 'I' and 'we'
love me
my love.

Love me my love
so that I don't give in
to the night.
Cope with my strangeness
so that I can
cope with me.

Love me
my love.

You have a new interpretation
for the lover's dreams.
You give a new definition
for the ancient version of
love.
You sing that
singing of you is breathing
and my self-forsaking
is my earning you.

You habited my heart
to die lovingly
to live for love
and to die in love.

Now that love's lament
is the need's cry
let madness welcome
which is my best remedy.
Love me
my love.

Love me
my love
although there is no time left
to be with you
although there is no respite
love me
my love.

Don't let me fall
stay with me
for I
won't reach my tomorrow
without you.

Love me
my love.

## Between The Snow And The Spring

And it is snowing
the village cock is sad
the village cock is silent
expectant young widows
knit hats for dead infants
in the village square
dogs lie in despair
at the feet of corpses
weeping

And wounded young men
bound in chains are hounded
by shadows and soldiers

The village cock crows
the expectant widows
make weapons for tomorrow's children
between the snow and the spring

And it is snowing.

## Night Square Sleepers

At night
when the dark skies know they must not cry
the square becomes a wide dormitory
rainless clouds make night sleepless
and I miss you.

As the last light dies
sullen pedlars,
shamefaced soldiers,
dark miners,
come with newspapers and dry coughs
smelling of smoke.
For a second
paper blankets, stuffed with news
press the huge weight of the world
on the crumpled bodies of
the night square sleepers.
Before leaving with wind.
And I miss you.

I miss you like a dark cloud
crying its heart out with pain.

A dark cloud cries out its heart
and the square awakes, wet with the night.
The wind has taken my paper away.
Yes, the old world will vanish with the wind.
And I miss you.
And dawn is raining.

### The Roof

I am thinking of a roof
a roof without cracks
a firm roof, stronger than steel
a firm roof to cover our fear
to clothe us on cold nights
a roof the size of our hearts
mine and yours
to feel the beat of anxiety.

Under this roof
with you
of flowers, of night and of the stars
I'll talk
of you and loving you
I'll say and say again
I'll measure my life with you
under this roof
and in you, I'll lose myself
to find new meaning

Alas! Our roof is the blanket of clouds
the horizon, and the infinity
our shortest distance
I am thinking of a roof
a dream roof, a roof for us

Even a cardboard roof
I am thinking of a roof
a roof with no cracks
a roof for love, for you and I.

A roof the size of our hearts
mine and yours
to feel the beat of anxiety
to shelter the privacy of mirrors
to catch the scent of petunias

Under this roof, if there is to be one
the scent of your body will linger
your dress will cover
the nakedness of its windows
under this roof
it's good to sprinkle the scent of self-forgetfulness
to sleep at the end of a story
and to get up at the start of a song.

Alas! Our roof is the blanket of clouds
the horizon, and the infinity
our shortest distance
I am thinking of a roof

## I Think Of Songs

I think
of the songs of sorrow
with their yellow melodies

O wheatless pastures
the naked deserts of blisters
beneath the hot skies
of my land
and the flash of the world's cloudburst
shines in my celestial eyes.

I think
of the songs of pain
with their violet melodies

O ruined homes
solitary cells on the lynched body
of my birthplace
and the molten torrents of the earth's volcanoes
burn from my ancient anger.

I think
of the songs of suffering
with their blue melodies

O uniformed children
sacrificed tomorrows on today's
slaughtering borders of my country
and the rage of rebellious slaves
of generations
rises in my historical throat

I think
of the songs of regret
with their green melodies

O faceless, bodiless girls
the lust robing flesh
on spread sheets
banished youth
of my native-land-mothers
and the caged birds of every century
fly to my loving heart

I think
of the songs of happiness
with their orange melodies
and the destitute of my land
wander through galaxies of sighs
with their cosmic poem-like fists
and together with the famished of the world
think of another rainbow

I think
of the songs of victory
with their purple melodies

# Leave to Remain

*For My Shahin*

**Leave to Remain** is a Film Four International/Spellbound Productions film, with the following cast:

| | |
|---|---|
| **Johnstone** | Jonathan Phillips |
| **Shahin** | Meda Kidem |
| **Henry** | Kazuko Hohki |
| **Javad** | Nasser Memarzia |
| **Ramdaad** | Sahand Meshcot |
| **Akbar** | Akbar Moein |
| **Ramin Arastafar** | Ali Kamrani |
| **Guran** | H Hamid |
| **Nasrin** | Zahra Jorjani |
| **Mina** | Georgia Clarke |
| **Nick** | William Gaminara |
| **Kalinowski** | Alfred Hoffman |
| **Ellen** | Alisa Bosschaert |
| **Woman at Home Office London** | Linda Bassett |
| **Dover** | David Bamber |
| **Embassy Official** | Amir Rima |
| **Mullah** | Paul Bentall |
| **Embassy Aide** | Mano Shada |
| **Raouf** | Steve Ashton |
| **Registrar** | Lavinia Bertram |
| **Photo Lab Assistant** | Anthony Milner |
| **Photographer** | Michael Hadley |
| **Bike Boy** | Barry Birch |
| **Immigration Officers** | Kit Jackson, David Millet, Steve Weston |
| **French Waiter** | Philippe Giraudeau |
| **Chicken Bar Assistant** | Christopher Simon |
| **Customer** | Steven O'Donnell |

*Directed by* Les Blair
*Director of Photography* Ivan Strasburg
*Music by* Simon Brint and Rowland Rivron
*Editor* Jon Gregory

*Pretitle Sequence*

*Darkness. A whistle, furtive. Footsteps moving over rough ground.*

*Slow scan of four Iranian faces: a young* **Girl,** *turned inwards, sobbing soundlessly; her* **Mother,** *eyes lowered, hair blown by a breeze; a* **Man,** *unshaven, head back, eyes closed; a* **Second Man,** *a little apart, alert, listening, his gaze fixed on the distance. He is shivering.*

*Shot of dawn sky, the sun rising behind mountains, high clouds moving west. A second whistle, nearer.*

*The* **Second Man** *moves to his right, out of a hollow in some rocks. He looks down through the darkness. Silence. Suddenly, the sound of a hand on a rifle. The* **Second Man** *whips round. Standing above the group is a dark faced man in Balouchi dress. He has a rifle slung on his shoulder, a cartridge belt across his chest. He looks at the anxious faces, smiles. He is their* **Guide.**

*The* **Guide** *leads the group down a steep slope in the gathering light. Behind him, the* **Man** *holds the* **Woman** *as she picks her way with care. At the rear, the* **Second Man** *carries the* **Girl.**

*The* **Guide** *stands on a rough dirt road. Half a mile ahead, an old flat-roofed building, a flag flying from the top. The sun has almost cleared the mountains, the light pushing towards the building. We hear the sound of the Azaan, high, distant.*

*The* **Second Man** *approaches the* **Guide.**

**Guide** (*pointing to the building*)  Pakistan.

*He unslings his rifle, holds out his hand. The* **Second Man** *quickly turns to the others, begins to collect their money. We see they wear city clothes.*

*Long shot from the roof of the building. On the edge of the frame, a* **Soldier** *stands facing the sun, his lower half in shot. As he sings the Azaan, we see the group moving along the road. The* **Soldier** *stamps his foot, once, twice. Beside him, the flag flutters in the breeze.*

*The* **Man** *lights a cigarette, exhales, moves up with the* **Woman** *and the* **Girl.**

*Behind them, thumbing his wad of notes, the* **Guide** *retraces his steps. Ahead, the* **Second Man** *leads the way to the border. As they approach, the Azaan stops. The* **Second Man** *quickens his pace. Suddenly, the* **Girl** *cries out.*

**Girl** (*O.O.S.*) Iran!

*The* **Second Man** *turns, sees the* **Girl** *pointing to the flag. He panics, starts to run back along the road. The others follow. Ahead, through the haze, a line of Iranian Guards appear. With a single movement, they release the catches on their machine guns.*

**Guard** (*in Farsi*) Freeze!

*The group freezes, the* **Second Man** *several yards in front. He looks either side of the road. There is no cover.*

**Woman** (*sensing he might run*) Jamshid. . .

*Suddenly, the other* **Man** *runs to his left, towards the mountains. A* **Guard** *swings round, opens fire. The* **Man** *drops, dead.*

*A* **Guard** *sits at a wooden table, a picture of Khomeini on the wall behind.* **Jamshid**, *the* **Woman** *and the* **Girl** *stand before him, handcuffed, their few possessions scattered acros the table: food, money, passports, a watch. A* **Second Guard** *tugs a wallet from* **Jamshid**'s *hip pocket. There's a photo on the outside, the image obscured by condensation under the plastic cover. The wallet is tossed onto the table.*

*The* **Guard** *fishes out the photo, looks at it, puts it on the table. As he goes through the wallet, we close on the photo: an Iranian woman, in western clothes, stands by the Serpentine in Kensington Gardens:* **Shahin.**

*Music up and Titles.*


*Interior: Lunar House, Croydon.*
*First Floor Landing – Day*

*A* **Black Porter**, *Home Office badge on his lapel, dispenses tickets from a battered machine to the queue of immigrants moving up the stairs. Beside him, a* **Woman**, *in her sixties, in nylon overall, an ID card pinned to her chest, sits clutching a cup of coffee. The* **Porter** *briefly questions people in turn, waves them through.* **Shahin**, *winter coat over elegant trouser suit, collects her ticket, passes into the visa hall. The* **Porter** *puts up his hand, looks down the stairs, assesses numbers, goes. The* **Woman** *moves across to guard the machine, sips her coffee.*


*Interior: Visa Hall – Day*

*A line of interview booths runs the length of the hall. From* **Shahin**'s

*P.O.V. we look along the digital display boards set at right angles to the booths. The numbers flip over, the tannoy crackles into life, people trudge up to the counter.* **Shahin** *sits on a bench at the end of the hall, away from the crowds, her distaste evident beneath the assumed composure. In front of her, a* **Libyan Man**, *in his forties, paces up and down smoking. A* **Second Libyan** *joins him. They argue, low, intense, in Arabic. Over this, the tannoy spills out fresh numbers.* **Shahin** *takes a newspaper from her bag, opens it:* The Times.

*Interior: Visa Hall – Day*

*We track from behind the booths taking in some of the morning's trade. A* **Moroccan Man**, *in his twenties, counts a wad of francs onto the counter; a* **Malaysian Woman** *confers with her sister in Tagalog; a* **Bangladeshi Man** *writes his address for a suspicious* **Officer**. *Forms are stamped, birth certificates checked, passports examined. Finally, we reach* **Shahin**. *She stands, impassive, as* **Edwards**, *a woman in her fifties, rapidly scans a two page letter.*

**Edwards** (*checking the signature*)  This is from your tutor?

**Shahin** *does not understand. She indicates a passage in the letter.*

**Shahin**  Please. He says. About the money.

**Edwards** (*reading*)  Yes, we know the problem. I don't quite see why he's written again. (*She turns to an open file.*) You've been sitting in on classes.

**Shahin** (*a prepared answer*)  It is important to keep up with my studies.

**Edwards** (*flicking through*)  Yes. Of course.

*She looks up.*

**Edwards**  Do you have a current bank statement?

**Shahin** *takes one from her bag, surrenders it.* **Edwards** *looks, sees what she expects, makes a note in the file.*

**Shahin** (*quiet, difficult*)  As a woman. You must understand. My country is no place for us.

**Edwards** *considers a reply, thinks better of it.*

**Edwards**  Miss Mohamedi. We must have proof of your ability to pay your fees. We can't wait another term. If the delay is with the authorities in Iran, I suggest you take up the matter with them.

*She stands, the ritual complete, picks up the file. A* **File Clerk***, black, in his forties, passes behind* **Edwards** *carrying a bundle of files.* **Edwards** *stops her, adds* **Shahin***'s to the pile.* **Shahin** *waits.*

**Edwards** (*turning*)  Was there something else dear?

**Shahin**  I have been here six years. My father is a rich man. There is no reason.

**Edwards** (*cool*)  We'll write.

*Interior: Train, Croydon to Victoria – Day*

*It's fairly full: blacks, indo-chinese among the blank faces.* **Shahin** *comes down the aisle, looking for a seat. Ahead, an* **Englishman***, in his forties, stands talking to a young* **Turk***. The* **Turk** *looks desperate, one hand on the* **Englishman***'s wrist.* **Shahin** *stops behind the* **Englishman***, unable to get past.*

**Turk** (*quiet, urgent*)  Fifty. Now. More when I get job.

*The* **Turk** *catches* **Shahin***'s eye, looks away. The* **Englishman** *turns, smiles.*

**Englishman**  Someone dropped their passport. Easily done. Perhaps –

*His hand goes to his inside pocket, waits.* **Shahin** *looks, pushes past.*

**Shahin**  Excuse me.

*Interior: Guard's Van – Day*

**Shahin** *turns into the guard's van, heading for the front of the train. We hear a flutter of wings. A pigeon hits the wire grid above* **Shahin***'s head. Startled, she stops, watches the bird as it hovers, then settles. Beyond it, an up-ended wicker basket, the lid open, 'Dover' chalked on the side. A trio of pigeons bob and peck across the floor.* **Shahin***, a hand at her throat, looks about for assistance, finds none, goes. The pigeon watches, blinks.*

*Interior: Fried Chicken Bar, Kensington – Day*

*A row of tables runs down one side of the 'L' shaped bar.* **Javad***, Iranian, late twenties, in appropriate outfit, works through a line of*

*take-away customers at the front: high street shoppers, tourists, kids.
Alongside,* **Ben,** *Libyan, a year or two younger, collects and bags
orders, energy flagging after the lunch-time rush. The tables are mostly
empty, littered with debris: cups, cartons abandoned meals.* **Henry,** *a
Chinese girl, late twenties, is clearing up mid-way down the bar, a
plastic sack in her hand. Music leaks from the walls, mushy
instrumental versions of Sinatra classics.*

**Javad** *holds up a restraining hand as an unshaven* **Italian** *attempts to
construct a meal that doesn't involve chicken.* **Javad** *leans over the side
of the bar, calls to* **Henry.**

**Javad**  Henry. We need chips.

**Henry** (*a wave*) Yeah, yeah.

*She carries on clearing tables.* **Javad** *snarls, shakes his head. He pulls
a paper cup from a dispenser, fills it with Coke.*

**Javad** (*to the* **Italian**) You look thirsty sir. Here. On the house.
(*He puts the Coke on the counter.*) Don't tell MacDonalds.

**Javad** *retreats to the kitchen. The* **Italian** *sheepishly sips the Coke,
sensing he's become a problem.*

**Shahin** *comes in the front of the bar, edges past the queue, finds*
**Henry.**

**Henry**  Wha' happen?

**Shahin**  The same. (*She sits, pulls a scarf from round her neck.*)
The train was so dirty. They treat you like children. Four
hours I waited.

**Henry**  Bloody Home Office. Nothing but send people home.
(*She scoops the rubbish from the table into her sack.*) You wanna eat?
Tea?

**Shahin**  Tea.

**Henry**  Smart move. Raouf cook today.

*She rolls her eyes.* **Shahin** *smiles.*

**Shahin**  Where is he?

**Henry** (*nods towards the back*) Fag.

**Shahin** *gets up, heads for the back.* **Henry** *crosses to another table,
trailing her sack.* **Javad,** *back at his post, gives her a questioning look.*
**Henry** *shakes her head.*

*Exterior: Rear of Chicken Bar – Day*

*A small yard opening onto an alley, a row of delivery bags on the other side.* **Raouf***, Nigerian, in his twenties, in company gear, sits on a low wall, his back to the open door. An extractor fan growls above his head. At his feet, a plain cardboard box, sealed with tape. He writes figures on a piece of paper, takes a pull on his Benson, begins to add.* **Shahin** *appears in the doorway, watches him a moment.*

**Shahin**  Busy?

**Raouf** (*startled*)  Jesus. Don't do that man. (*He stands, pockets the paper.*) Mr Englishman come this morning. Wants me move to Brixton. You know Brixton? (**Shahin** *nods.*) What they want to move a black man to Brixton for. It's full of black men. I'm just gettin' organised here.

*He takes a last pull on his fag, flicks away the butt, gazes along the alley.* **Shahin** *waits, uncertain of his mood.*

**Shahin**  I need to see your friend.

**Raouf** (*turning*)  Yeah?

**Shahin**  Today.

**Raouf** *looks at her, sees she means it.*

**Raouf**  Sure. I gotta catch someone. (*A glance at the box.*) Coupla minutes. (**Shahin** *turns to go.*) Hey. You eaten? I cook today.

**Shahin** (*moving, kisses her fingers*)  Perfect.

**Raouf** *resumes his watch, beaming.*

*Interior: Chicken Bar, Kitchen Area – Day*

*A metal table butts onto the chicken freezer.* **Shahin** *puts her bag on the work-top, rests her back against the edge. Behind her, a Singapore Airlines calendar displays a smiling stewardess. The days have been neatly crossed off.* **Javad** *and* **Ben** *are still serving at the front. Down from them,* **Henry** *bales chips from the fryer. She dumps her haul, brings* **Shahin** *a cup of tea.*

**Henry**  Wha' you gonna do?

**Shahin** (*taking it*)  I can't wait Henry. I have to get visa. Work.

*She blows on her tea, sips.*

**Henry** Wha' about college?

**Shahin** How can I study? They won't let me borrow books.

**Henry** So you can work now. You don't need visa.

*She takes two N.I. cards from her pocket, selects one, hands it to* **Shahin. Shahin** *takes it, reads the name.*

**Shahin** This is a *man*, Henry.

**Henry** Yeah. So's this. (*She waves the other card.*) Doesn't matter. Woman is nothing in Iran. You told me. Sit inside all day. Wear veil. Your face too pretty for this. You need nice red uniform. (*She indicates her own.*) Very sexy.

**Shahin** I couldn't. Thank you, but no. I didn't come here to hide. I want to be me, not – (*She looks along the kitchen.*) Anyway, I can't cook.

*She hands back the card.* **Henry** *looks at it, sniffs.*

**Henry** Raouf can't cook. Nobody notice.

**Shahin** Henry. Please. It's too dangerous. There would be questions. (**Henry** *takes the card, pockets it.*) You bring my bag?

**Henry** Yeah, I bring your bag. (*She heaves a black travel bag from under the table, puts it on top.*) You didn't say it full of brick. Chinese people is very small, Shahin.

**Shahin** *takes a Pentax camera from the bag, starts to unload the film.* **Henry** *watches, milkshake in hand.*

**Shahin** You drink too much.

**Henry** It's strawberry. Makes me feel nice. (*She nods at the camera.*) Who's this for?

**Shahin** (*not the first time*) He's Iranian. An estate agent. He finds flats for all the poor people who have nowhere to go. And a few rich ones. No one needs to know.

**Henry** And?

**Shahin** *pops the film into a plastic canister, avoiding the question. She shrugs.*

**Shahin** It'll be good practice. One day, I take your picture for Vogue.

**Shahin** *pockets the film, bags the camera.* **Henry** *waits for more, not impressed.*

**Shahin** (*finally*) He has a friend.

**Henry** A man.

**Shahin** Yes.

**Henry** English.

**Shahin** (*zipping up*) I don't want to argue. I've made up my mind.

**Henry** You're crazy, Shahin. You don't have to do this.

**Raouf** *comes through the back door, a bottle of vodka in his hand, stands next to* **Shahin.**

**Raouf** She complaining 'bout me?

**Shahin** No, it's me. She thinks I should wash dishes.

**Raouf** Easy money. We ain't got any. (*He gives* **Henry** *the vodka.*) You know what she do with this? (*Whispers.*) Milkshake. . .

**Henry** Shut up, Raouf.

**Raouf** *and* **Shahin** *laugh.* **Henry** *scowls, hides the bottle.*

**Raouf** (*to* **Shahin**) Come on.

*He goes.* **Shahin** *shoulders her bag, looks along the bar towards* **Javad.**

**Shahin** (*to* **Henry**) When's Javad finish?

**Henry** He's going to airport. Mina's here.

*A beat.* **Shahin** *takes in the news.*

**Shahin** From Iran? I thought – has she heard anything? About Jamshid?

**Raouf** *calls from the back.* **Shahin** *hesitates.*

**Henry** She's not here yet. Go. Ring Javad later.

**Henry** *shoos her away.* **Shahin** *goes.* **Henry** *ambles up to the fryer, joins* **Javad.**

**Javad** Anything new?

**Henry** *drags the scoop through the oil, nets a stray chip.*

**Henry** She's gonna get married.

*Exterior: Cinema/Alleyway – Day*

**Raouf** *leads* **Shahin** *down the side of the cinema. They enter the building through a rear door marked 'No Entry', move along a gloomy corridor.* **Raouf** *opens a door set flush in the corridor wall. Inside, a* **Filipino Man** *sits on a bench eating peaches from a can. He wears an usher's jacket. Other jackets hang from pegs on the wall.*

**Raouf** *(changing jackets)* Where's Isa?

**Filipino** *(intent on a peach)* Out front.

**Raouf** *(pointing to the can)* They're South African man.

*He takes some cards from his chicken jacket, slips them into his top pocket, motions* **Shahin** *to follow. The* **Filipino** *spears a slice, eats.*

*Interior: Cinema/Foyer – Day*

*The front doors are locked, the lights unlit.* **Raouf** *emerges from behind a curtain, followed by* **Shahin. Isa** *stands with another* **Filipino Girl** *by the box office.*

**Raouf** Wait here.

**Shahin** *stands by the wall. Behind her, a poster for Olympic Sun Tours. She watches* **Raouf** *cross to* **Isa***, confer. He takes the cards from his pocket, gives them to* **Isa***. **Isa** *looks at the* **Cinema Manager** *taking the chains off the doors, moves to the Ladies' Toilet.* **Raouf** *signals* **Shahin** *to follow.*

*Interior: Ladies' Toilet – Day*

*Daylight through two narrow windows set high in the wall. Inside the door, an electric hand-dryer. A mirror above the fitted wash-basins.*

**Isa** Trouble, yeah? Is OK. *(She sits on the wash-basin surround.)* You got 10p?

**Shahin** *looks in her coat pocket, finds one.*

**Shahin** Here.

**Isa** *produces* **Raouf**'s *cards: lottery tickets. She rubs the hidden symbols* *with the edge of the coin as she talks.*

**Isa**  Best place Englishman Tropicana. Big disco. Plenty men. Dance. Buy drink. One time, two time you find man. (*She's got through a couple of cards.*) Aiee. Ace. You watch, all the same. I get King win ten thousand pound.

**Shahin**  How much did you pay?

**Isa**  My husband? He's crazy 'bout movies. (*She grins.*) Bargain huh? (*She starts on another card.*) You got boyfriend?

**Shahin** *doesn't reply.* **Isa** *looks at her in the mirror.*

**Shahin**  Did they visit? The Home Office.

**Isa**  Na. Too busy with holiday. We marry in summer. (*She looks gloomily at her cards, slips off the ledge hands back the coin.*) You want disco with us?

**Shahin**  No. It's not that. (*She lowers her eyes.*) I have someone.

**Isa**  What's problem?

*The door is knocked, the* **Manager** *calls.* **Isa** *groans, goes to the hand-dryer, thumps the button, opens the door a fraction.*

**Isa**  (*behind the door; shouts*)  Dry hands.

*The* **Manager** *retreats, muttering.* **Isa** *lets the door close.*

**Isa**  Men is so dumb. (*She feels* **Shahin**'s *coat.*) Nice. What you do?

**Shahin**  It was a present.

*They look at each other.* **Isa** *raises a quizzical eyebrow.* **Shahin** *smiles, nods.*

**Isa**  You miss him?

**Shahin**  I don't know where he is. He went back to Iran. (*She picks at the coat.*) He wanted to try and do something. He's very impatient.

**Isa**  Like you.

**Shahin**  (*smiles*)  Like me.

**Isa**  (*serious, practical*)  Visa takes two, three months. It's not too bad. Can be fun with right man. Don't marry Kensington. Go Fulham, Chelsea. Put few men's things in room. Just in case.

(*She takes a ring from her finger.*) Here. This one lucky. (*She holds out the ring,* **Shahin** *looks at it.*) I didn't sleep with him.

**Shahin** *takes the ring, leaves.*


*Exterior: Kensington Mews – Day*

*A narrow cobblestoned cul-de-sac, packing boxes, rubbish sacks littering the alley. On both sides, cramped offices and depots, import agencies in the main: tea, antiques, textiles. At the far end, a commercial photographic lab above a coffee importer's, iron stairs leading to the entrance. On the left, a Persian carpet warehouse, the loading bay door swung up, half-open. An* **Iranian Storeman**, *grey overalls, woolly hat, crawls from under the door rolling a carpet out across the mews.*

**Shahin** *turns into the alley, makes for the lab, reaches the carpet. The* **Storeman** *sees her, sits back on his heels. He takes off his hat, clutches it to his chest, invites her to walk over it.* **Shahin** *smiles, tip-toes across, admired by the* **Storeman.**


*Interior: Photographic Lab – Day*

**Shahin** *fills in a form at the counter, her bag next to her, a film canister in her hand. Across from her, by the window, a* **Photographer**, *English, in his thirties, clips a sheet of transparencies to a light box hung on the wall. The drone of the processing machines fills the tiny space.*

*A* **Lab Assistant**, *female, in her twenties, worn out by a tedious day, comes to the counter, takes* **Shahin**'s *film, looks at the form.*

**Assistant**  Normal?

**Shahin** *nods.*

**Assistant**  Normal. (*She alters the form.*) Just tick the box.

*She punches a timed ticket from the digital dispenser on the counter, hands it over.*

**Assistant**  Two hours.

**Photographer** (*O.O.S.*)  Is this thing working?

**Assistant** (*moving off, mumbles*)  Try hitting it.

**Photographer** (*to* **Shahin**)  What she say?

**Shahin** *shoulders her bag, goes to the light box.*

**Shahin** Here.

*She smacks the side of the box with the flat of her hand. The light
blinks on. We see the transparencies: a sequence of wedding pictures —
bride, groom, marriage guests assembled outside a parish church.*


*Interior: Kensington Market,* **Bamdaad**'s *office — Day*

*From* **Shahin**'s *P.O.V. we look out along the narrow passage between
stalls. The market is closing, lights blink off, the last stalls are boarded
up. A few* **Stall Workers**, *mainly women, hurry towards us making
for the stairs. As the last light goes, we see a* **Man**'s *image reflected in
the glass:* **Johnstone**.

*Johnstone, twenty-four, slight, streaked hair, wearing a knee-length
overcoat, the collar turned up. He has an earing in his left ear. He
emerges from the back of the office in front of* **Bamdaad**, *Iranian, late
forties, greying hair, good suit.* **Bamdaad** *has* **Shahin**'s *envelope of
transparencies in his hand.*

**Bamdaad** Miss Mohamedi. This is my very good friend, Mr
Johnstone.

**Shahin** *nods.* **Johnstone** *rubs his hands, preparing for a handshake
that never arrives.*

**Bamdaad** (*brisk*) Please, please. (*He invites them to sit.*) I told Mr
Johnstone you have problem. He say, no problem. He is
English.

*He smiles, sits. On the wall behind a framed picture of the* **Shah**.
*Underneath, several flyers for flats, the details in Farsi, the interiors
illustrated.*

Unfortunately, Mr Johnstone has no work. But Allah ho akbar.
(*He gestures to the heavens.*) He has a house in Chelsea, a rich
family. He is very kind. And he likes Iranian. (*A joke.*) But not
Khomeini.

**Johnstone** It's a squat.

**Shahin** *frowns, looks to* **Bamdaad**. **Bamdaad** *is looking through
**Shahin**'s pictures, holding them to the light.*

It's not my house. It's just a place we use.

**Bamdaad** In Chelsea.

**Johnstone** Yeah.

**Bamdaad**  This is the main thing. I know property, Mr Johnstone. This is my business.

**Johnstone** (*to* **Shahin**)  There's no carpets or anything. . .

**Shahin**  Please. It is not important. My husband will live in my house.

**Johnstone** *deals with the unexpected news, turns to* **Bamdaad.**

**Bamdaad** (*studying the pictures*)  This is not necessary, I think.

**Johnstone**  I don't mind. I'll sleep anywhere. Stand in the sink if you like. (*He waits for a response, gets none.*) Where d'you live?

**Shahin**  I was in Kensington. Now, Notting Hill.

**Johnstone**  I've seen you around, I think. Sundays. Down by the Embassy.

**Shahin**  No. I don't go there.

*She stiffens a little, exchanges a look with* **Bamdaad. Johnstone** *catches the concern.*

**Johnstone**  I said something wrong?

**Bamdaad**  Embassy is bad place, Mr Johnstone. Always making trouble. Spying on people. We do not like it. We want to be like you. Free to do as we please.

*He gets up, calls over his shoulder.*

**Bamdaad**  Davoud! (*To* **Shahin**, *in Farsi.*) You gave me Hyde Park Mansions.

**Shahin** *goes to the desk, shows him the sheet.*

**Shahin** (*in Farsi*)  That's it.

**Bamdaad** (*in Farsi*)  Ah yes. Good. (*He shuffles the sheets together.*) I think we can do business. Pay him cash. I'll discount my fee against these. (*He glances at the invoice.*) That leaves one hundred.

**Shahin** (*in Farsi*)  We agreed one fifty.

**Bamdaad** (*a gesture, in Farsi*)  Englishmen are hard to find.

**Shahin** *hesitates, aware of* **Johnstone** *watching.*

**Shahin** (*in Farsi*)  There will be more work?

**Bamdaad** (*in Farsi*) There is always more work.

**Bamdaad** *goes to* **Johnstone**, *hand extended.*

Goodbye Mr Johnstone. Iranian people owe you a great debt. I hope you have a very pleasant evening.

*And he's gone. An awkward silence.*

**Johnstone** (*indicating the picture*) Who's that?

**Shahin** This is Shah.

**Johnstone** Oh yeah.

**Davoud** *appears: Iranian, in his twenties, jeans and parka, a suitcase in his hand. He winks at* **Johnstone**, *hands him the case. It's covered in travel stickers: Sealink, KLM, British Airways, Transalpino, etc.*

**Johnstone** (*taking it*) Jesus. Forget me head.

**Davoud** *beckons them to follow.*


*Interior: Ground Floor, Kensington Market – Day*

**Shahin** *and* **Johnstone** *move along the narrow passage between stalls. It's dark, blue night-lights feeble against the black walls.* **Shahin** *leads the way. Ahead, the sound of* **Davoud**'s *footsteps making for the exit.* **Shahin** *takes a wrong turning, stops, unsure of the way.*

**Shahin** (*to herself, in Farsi*) Where's he gone.

**Davoud** *whistles.* **Shahin** *turns towards the sound. A metal shutter is pulled up on the lights of Kensington, the soft roar of traffic.* **Shahin** *and* **Johnstone** *go to the exit, pass out into the night.* **Davoud** *pulls down the shutter. His footsteps echo in the dark. He starts to sing.*


*Interior: Fried Chicken Bar – Day*

**Henry**, *smart slacks and jumper, a coat over her arm, clatters towards us down the side of the bar in a pair of high heels. A few solitary customers sit hunched over their food.* **Henry** *stops next to* **Ben**, *intent on making tea, slips into her coat.*

**Henry** (*impatient*) Where's Raouf?

**Ben** Go. I can manage. (*He puts the tea on the counter, nods across the bar.*) Seen that?

**Henry** *looks. From her P.O.V. we see* **Shahin***, her back to the bar, sitting opposite* **Johnstone***, the remains of a meal between them.* **Johnstone** *is showing* **Shahin** *selected highlights from his case, holds out something for her to inspect.*

**Henry** (*taking the tea*) This hers?

**Ben** *nods.* **Henry** *goes to the table, puts the cup in front of* **Shahin***.* **Shahin** *examines a tie in a cellophane wrapper.*

**Henry** (*sweetly*) Good evening sir, Good evening, madam. Your tea. (*She takes the tie from* **Shahin***, studies it.*) Wha's this?

*She looks at* **Johnstone***. He senses an opportunity to impress.*

**Johnstone** Want one? I was just telling – (*He gestures at* **Shahin***.*) Three for a quid. Have a look. I'm gonna give it a go up Oxford Street. Fleece the tourists.

*He opens his case. Inside, a display of ties, neatly stacked in wrappers, clearly destined to remain there.*

**Henry** You sell these things?

**Johnstone** (*casual*) Yeah, sometimes.

*He grins at* **Shahin***.* **Shahin** *looks away, a hand at her mouth.*

**Henry** You're crazy, mister. Nobody want this. (*She tosses the tie into the case, smacks the lid.*) And you got funny hair. (*To* **Shahin***, on the move.*) Lucky I was here. You buy anything.

*She hits* **Shahin***'s shoulder, a playful reproof, goes.* **Johnstone***, floored, labours to stay in the race.*

**Johnstone** It's just a casual arrangement. Hobby, really. I don't – (*He runs a hand over his hair.*) She a friend of yours or something?

**Shahin** I come here. Few times. Yes.

**Johnstone** I look alright, don't I?

**Shahin** Yes. Of course. (*She looks down, pulling away from the intimacy.*) I thought if I paid something.

**Johnstone** What, a deposit?

**Shahin** (*evasive*) It may not be necessary to marry. I don't know.

**Johnstone**  Look, if you don't like me –

**Shahin**  No. Please. You're –

*She searches for the word.*

**Johnstone**  Blonde, blue-eyed and handsome. Yeah, they all say that. I'm part Scandinavian. Never offer me a pint of lager. (*He drops his voice.*) You on the run?

**Shahin** (*smiles, shakes her head*)  I can't pay my fees. The money is from my father. The ministry won't let him send it.

**Johnstone** (*nods*)  Stopped your giro. Know the feeling.

*A small silence.* **Shahin** *makes a decision, takes an envelope from her pocket, puts it on the table.* **Johnstone** *looks at it, struggles with the temptation to investigate, gives in.* **Shahin** *weighs his reaction.*

**Johnstone**  I don't get it. How much are your fees?

**Shahin**  I have money to live or money to study. Not both. I must go.

*She stands, gathers her belongings.*

**Johnstone**  Any chance of a lift? Car's off the road.

**Shahin**  I have to see some friends. (*She offers her hand.*) Thank you for the evening.

*They shake.* **Shahin** *goes, heads for the back entrance.* **Johnstone** *watches, pops a nugget in his mouth, chews.*

*Interior:* **Javad**'s *Council Flat, Hallway – Dusk*

*A half-open door along the unlit corridor, one or two faces lit by the flickering glare of a TV, the sound in Farsi.* **Akbar**, *Iranian, in his thirties, loose shirt over dark cords, appears from the kitchen, a sheaf of papers in his hands. He opens the front door, grunts in surprise as* **Shahin** *steps into the hall.*

**Shahin** (*in Farsi*)  I can't stay long.

**Akbar** (*in Farsi*)  He's in there. Mind the bags.

*He indicates a pile of luggage stacked by a door on the right: hold-all, shoulder bag, flight bag.* **Shahin** *moves along the hall.*

**Akbar** (*in Farsi*)  Hey. (**Shahin** *turns.*) Come and talk.

**Shahin** nods, slips into the living room. **Akbar** retreats to the kitchen.

Interior: **Javad**'s Flat/Living Room – Dusk

**Javad**, two or three Iranian students, and **Nick**, English, in his thirties, jeans and trainers, donkey jacket bundled on his lap, sit on the floor watching **Javad**'s video. Beyond them, two mattresses with improvised bedding, a student, flat out, a bottle of Pils clamped to his chest. **Mina**, an Iranian woman in her twenties, sits on a chair, apart from the group. She smokes, toying with the cigarette, not watching the video.

**Shahin** unbuttons her coat, leans against the wall by the door, her eyes on the video.

Heads turn, **Javad** waves, motions her to join them on the floor. **Shahin** signals she's fine. From her P.O.V. we watch the video: Kurdish guerrillas, men and women, assemble in a mountain village, are briefed by their commander.

**Shahin** watches **Mina** from the shadows. **Mina** pulls on her cigarette, stares at the floor. The students gives a muted cheer as the guerrillas fool for the camera. **Mina** looks up at **Shahin**, blank, tired, her eyes old. She grabs her pack of Marlborough, heads for the hall, hand on her back. As she passes, her fag-end brushes **Shahin**'s coat, the tip dropping to the floor. **Mina** stops, puts a hand on **Shahin**'s arm.

**Mina** (in Farsi) Excuse me. . .

She goes. **Shahin** stamps out the burning ash, follows **Mina** down the hall, wanting to talk. **Mina**, oblivious, enters the room by the luggage, closes the door. **Shahin** hesitates, glances through the kitchen door at **Akbar**, papers in hand, holding forth to a **Woman** sewing a dress at an electric machine. **Shahin** goes to the front door, slips out.

Exterior: **Javad**'s Flat/Walkway – Dusk

**Shahin** looks out across the housing estate, the flat door open behind her. A dog barks, reggae thumps in the distance. In the yard below, a **Girl** laughs, chased by a **Boy** advancing through the shadows. **Shahin** watches as the **Girl**, sixteen or so, is caught, starts to protest, the game turning sour.

**Javad** (O.O.S.) It's cold.

**Shahin** turns as **Javad** and **Nick** emerge from the flat.

**Javad**  This is Nick. He's going to write a letter for Mina.

**Nick** *smiles.* **Shahin** *nods.*

**Shahin** (*to* **Javad**)  What happened?

**Javad**  They said in Stockholm she must apply here. (*He shrugs.*) So.

**Shahin**  Is she alright?

**Nick**  She's got a good case. I can't see there'll be any problems.

**Shahin**  Her friends are in Stockholm.

**Nick**  Oh. I'm sorry. I just assumed.

**Shahin** (*to* **Javad**)  Is there any news?

**Javad** *shakes his head.* **Shahin** *looks at the ground a moment.*

**Shahin** (*moving*)  I'll miss the bus.

**Javad** (*in Farsi*)  You working for Bamdaad?

**Shahin** *stops, turns.*

**Shahin** (*in Farsi, slow*)  He's helping me. Yes.

**Javad** (*in Farsi*)  This man is rubbish, Shahin. A bourgeois. For years they sit on their suitcases. As soon as trouble begins, they leave. We must keep together.

**Shahin** (*in Farsi*)  I don't want to argue.

**Javad** (*in Farsi*)  And Jamshid?

**Shahin** (*in Farsi*)  Jamshid's in Iran.

**Javad** (*in Farsi*)  You don't know.

**Shahin** (*in Farsi, hard*)  No. I don't. Six months I've waited. Nothing. Not one letter. Do you know what that feels like?

*She stares at him.* **Javad** *drops his head, weary of the old argument.* **Nick,** *caught in the flak, makes to escape.*

**Nick**  I'll leave you to it.

*He edges past* **Javad.** **Shahin** *stops him.*

**Shahin**  No. Stay. If you want to help us you must learn about Iranian people. Javad is a revolutionary.

**Javad** Oh Shahin...

**Shahin** (*through him*) That is why he stands here talking politics while his wife sits in kitchen making dresses. You know how much she is paid? By her *bourgeois* boss? One pound. Each dress. One pound. (*She pauses, the anger spent.*) Khomeini's in Iran too Javad. Not here. We have to make a life where we are.

*She goes.* **Nick** *puffs his cheek.*

**Nick** Wow.

**Javad** You should see her when she's angry.

*Interior:* **Shahin**'s *Flat, Kitchen – Night*

*Shot of an electric samovar, hot water gushing through the narrow tap into a china teapot.* **Shahin**, *her coat on, enters the frame, unclasps her hair, flips off the tap, searches vainly for a glass.*

**Henry** (*O.O.S.*) 'bove sink.

**Henry**, *knee-length baseball shirt, woollen socks, leans against the door frame, a bottle of wine in her hand. She looks flushed, tousled. Beyond her, the living room is in darkness.*

**Shahin** (*sighs*) I hate this kitchen. It's so small. In Kensington I had...

**Henry** ... bigger cupboards. You told me. Every day ten weeks you told me.

**Shahin** (*smiles*) Am I always complaining?

*She reaches above the sink, finds a glass.*

**Henry** It's your flat. I'm just lodger.

**Shahin** (*pouring tea*) I pay rent too, Henry.

**Henry** *runs the neck of the bottle across her lips, studies* **Shahin**'s *quiet insistence.*

**Henry** I don't like him.

**Shahin** *dips a finger in her tea, tastes it, adds water.*

**Shahin** He's English.

**Henry** (*fond*) Shahin. You can't just... Men can be difficult. They not like us.

**Shahin** You think I don't know this? What am I supposed to do? Go dancing?

**Henry** You might enjoy it.

**Shahin** I don't ask permission, Henry. Not yours. Not Javad's.

*She pushes past into the darkness of the living room, sits on the sofa.* **Henry** *waits by the door.*

**Shahin** Every week, my father goes to ministry in Tehran. To ask about my money. And every week they give same answer. Estebah showdeh. It's a mistake. My papers are lost. They'll write. Just like Home Office. (*She looks across at* **Henry**.) They're *playing* with me, Henry. Because I'm a woman. Because they don't like what I study. I don't know. (*She pauses, swills her tea.*) I won't play this game. I want my own life. If that means. . .

*She shrugs, drinks her tea.* **Henry** *is not impressed.*

**Henry** You must be important person if Khomeini do this. He's busy man.

**Shahin** *smiles, despite herself, cut down to size.*

**Shahin** I know, I know. I'm just a poor rich girl who doesn't want to work in kitchen.

**Henry** (*innocent*) I didn't say anything.

*A small silence.* **Henry** *toys with the bottle.*

**Shahin** I'll need the room.

**Henry** When?

**Shahin** A few weeks. I'm not sure. I have enough money for two, three months. Longer if I'm careful.

**Henry** *waits, not helping.*

**Shahin** (*quiet*) I didn't know Jamshid in Iran. I've never seen his house, his family. I know the street. There's trees. A fruit shop. But I can't picture him there. That's what makes it so hard, not knowing where he is. I imagine all the places I've been. Shahsavar. Esfahan. The hills outside the city. But he doesn't come.

**Henry** *pushes herself off the wall, pads across to the sofa, sits.*

**Henry** (*finally*) You're right. It's a horrible flat.

**Shahin** *turns to her, grateful.*

**Shahin** What will you do?

**Henry** This is my third in six month. I'll move. What you think I do?

*She rolls her eyes.* **Shahin** *laughs.* **Henry** *puts her arm round her, offers her the bottle.*

**Henry** Come. Have a drink. Just you and me.

*The bedroom doors opens behind them. A* **Chinese Man***, in his twenties, shorts, bare chest, appears in the doorway.*

**Man** (*in Chinese*) Li? What you doing?

*He rubs his eyes.* **Henry** *groans.*

**Shahin** It's alright. (*She gets up.*) I have to sleep.

**Shahin** *nods at the* **Man***, embarrassed by his nakedness, slips into her bedroom. The* **Man** *joins* **Henry** *on the sofa, tries for a kiss.* **Henry** *pushes him in the chest, growls, clutches her bottle.*

*Interior:* **Shahin***'s Bedroom, 1 a.m. – Night*

**Shahin** *pulls back a curtain hung across a small recess, snaps on an anglepoise. Behind the curtain, a make-shift worktable, basic photographic equipment stacked at one end: enlarger, trays, chemicals. Pinned to the wall above the table, several prints:* **Shahin***'s parents, various Iranian landscapes, one or two interiors.*

*There are no pictures of* **Shahin***, but several of* **Jamshid***.*

**Shahin** *sits on a stool in her nightdress. Beyond her, we see her bed has already been slept in. She rubs her face, picks up an air-mail pad lying on the table, a half-written letter in Farsi on the top. Through the wall we hear* **Henry** *and the* **Man** *laughing and shushing each other.* **Shahin** *reads the letter, gives up, tears off the page, discards it. She looks at* **Jamshid***'s picture on the wall. The light clicks off.*

*Exterior: (Dream) – Dawn*

*A figure runs towards us up a rough mountain track in the murky dawn light. As it comes nearer, we see it is* **Shahin***. She wears a cream jacket and trousers, red shoes; her hair is loose, a camera slung over her shoulder. She stumbles as she runs, her heels catching on stones.*

*Ahead, two women, in black chadors, their faces covered, squat by the roadside. One of them holds a picture frame in her lap, the image obscured by sunlight glinting on the glass. On the hill behind them, a* **Man** *stands facing the sun. As* **Shahin** *approaches the women, the sound fades up. The* **Man** *sings the Azaan.*

*Exterior: Registry Office Car Park – Day*

*An empty mini-cab, amber lights flashing, parked on the kerb, the driver's window open. At the back of the shot a young man in morning suit, a carnation in his lapel, stands smoking a cigarette. We hear a voice on the mini-cab radio attempting contact.*

**Radio**  One Eight, One Eight. One of your lot for Heathrow, over. (*Pause.*) One eight, One eight. (*Pause.*) Come on you daft bastard, what're you doing out there. . . ?

*Interior: Registry Office – Day*

*The hexagonal marriage hall. High windows, fitted carpets, concealed lighting – civic interior design attempting style.*

**Raouf, Johnstone, Shahin** and **One Eight**, *an Iranian in his thirties are lined up before the* **Registrar**, *a white haired man, in his fifties, confronting his fourth marraige of the afternoon with minimal enthusiasm.* **Miss Davis**, *the* **Registrar**'s *assistant, stands to one side.* **Johnstone** *uncomfortable in a borrowed suit, clutches* **Shahin**'s *hand.*

**Registrar**  Do you take Shahin Mohamedi. . .

**Johnstone**  Do you take Shahin Momd. . .

*He eyes the* **Registrar** *warily; the* **Registrar** *glances at his card.*

**Registrar**  Mohamedi. . .

**Johnstone** (*quiet*)  Sorry.

**Registrar**  No, no. Just repeat the oath.

**Johnstone**  Do you take Shahin. . . ? (*He looks down.*) . . . Christ.

*The group stirs uneasily. The* **Registrar** *flicks his card.* **One Eight** *leans into* **Johnstone**.

**One Eight**  Mo-ham-ed-di. (*To* **Registrar**.) Very difficult for English.

**Registrar**  Please Mr. . .

**One Eight**  Ramin Arastafar.

**Registrar**  Would you not interrupt.

**Johnstone**  I've not done this before.

**Raouf** *laughs, suddenly amused. The* **Registrar** *waits for silence.* **Miss Davis** *looks on, fascinated.*

**Registrar**  Perhaps we should go back to the beginning. Now that everyone's relaxed.

*He musters his dignity.* **Shahin** *gives* **Johnstone** *an encouraging smile.*

*Interior: Registry Office – Day*

*Close up of the marriage register.* **Shahin**'s *hand enters the frame, slowly writers her name next to* **Johnstone**'s *in the ledger. Over this:*

**Registrar**  Well I think I can say that's the longest wedding I've performed this week. A good sign, I'm sure.

**Shahin** *stands with* **Johnstone. One Eight,** *car keys at the ready, and* **Raouf,** *baffled by the small talk, look on.* **Miss Davis** *hands* **Shahin** *the marriage certificate.*

**Miss Davis**  There we are.

*The wedding party murmur their thanks, leave,* **Shahin** *and* **Johnstone** *in the lead. The* **Registrar** *watches them go, turns to* **Miss Davis.**

**Registrar** *(dry)*  Kind of the Home Office to keep us busy.

**Miss Davis**  Perhaps you should write and thank them.

*The* **Registrar** *looks down at the register, purses his lips.*

*Exterior: Street/Interior, Mini Cab – Day*

**Raouf,** *laughing with relief, is changing into his chicken bar uniform in the front passenger seat.* **One Eight,** *radio mike in hand, calls his base as he speeds towards Kensington. In the rear,* **Johnstone,** *tie loose, lies back in his seat next to* **Shahin.** *His eyes are closed.*

**One Eight**  One Eight, One Eight. Clearing Beechwood Road. Over. . .

**Radio**  Afternoon Sinbad. What're you trying to do. Starve?

You're supposed to be on a mercy dash to Heathrow. . .

**Raouf** (*over this*) I thought we never get outta there. You see his face. Lord above. That guy beat his wife every day of the week. (*He looks at* **Johnstone**.) He OK?

**Shahin** He's fine.

*Exterior: Rear of Chicken Bar – Day*

**Mina**, *in chicken bar uniform and hat, stands by the back door of the shop, looking along the alley. The mini-cab appears,* **One Eight** *toots the horn.* **Mina** *waves, goes inside.*

**Raouf** *leaps out the front of the cab, disappears inside the shop, returns with several plastic bags of food.* **Henry**, *out of uniform, follows him, a milkshake carton in one hand, a large parcel under her arm.* **Raouf** *dumps the bags in the front seat.* **Henry** *goes to* **Johnstone**'*s side, taps the window.* **Johnstone** *winds it down, is handed the milkshake carton.*

**Henry** You look after Shahin, Henry look after you. You give us trouble, we kill you.

*She smiles sweetly, goes round to the front of the cab.* **Javad** *and* **Mina** *appear at the back door.* **Henry** *calls to them.*

Bye bye children.

*She drops into the car, shuts the door. The cab lurches forward, stalls.* **Ben** *joins* **Javad**, **Mina** *and* **Raouf** *at the back door,* **Raouf** *giving the others the story.* **One Eight** *re-starts the engine, roars off. The bar staff wave,* **Mina** *and* **Ben** *quickly going back inside.* **Raouf** *turns to* **Javad**.

**Raouf** You wanna go?

**Javad** Later.

**Raouf** Surprised?

**Javad** (*shakes his head*) She thinks she's in England.

*Exterior: Street/Interior: Mini Cab – Day*

**Shahin** *sits with* **Henry**'*s parcel open on her lap: two men's suits, obviously not new, a shirt and tie.* **Johnstone** *sipping his milkshake, looks on, curious. In the front,* **Henry**, *notebook in hand, checks the* *afternoon's agenda.*

**Henry** Don't ask where they come from. You don't see me again, ring police, tell them arrest man in my flat with no clothes on. (*She looks at* **Shahin**, *grins, nods at* **Johnstone**.) Whose is that?

**One Eight** Mine.

**Henry** (*disbelief*) You wear this?

**One Eight** *nods,* **Henry** *gets the giggles.*

**Johnstone** (*to* **Shahin**) Have I got to change again or something?

*Interior:* **Shahin**'s *Flat, Living Room – Day*

*Three Iranians –* **Akbar, Guran, Nazarine** – *launch into the chorus of wedding song.* **One Eight**, **Johnstone**'s *suitcase at his feet, claps in tempo.* **Henry**, *tray in hand, distributes glasses of champagne, wailing her own traditional greeting to newly-weds. The song ends to a splatter of applause.* **Shahin** *turns to* **Johnstone**, *offers to clink glasses.* **Johnstone** *obliges, then drinks from his milkshake carton. Everyone drinks, except* **Shahin**.

**Shahin** This is James. (*She introduces the guests.*) Guran, Akbar, Nazarine.

**Johnstone** *nods, shakes hands with* **Akbar**. *He holds up his milk-shake carton.*

**Johnstone** Cheers. Hands across the ocean.

*Silence.* **One Eight** *lifts the case.* **Henry** *retreats to the kitchen.*

**One Eight** (*to* **Johnstone**) Where to sir?

**Johnstone** *looks to* **Shahin**.

**Shahin** Just leave it there.

**Akbar** (*in Farsi*) So, Ramin, you're moving in too?

**One Eight** (*in Farsi*) You know us bloody foreigners. Always sleep four in the bed. My father and uncle are coming this evening. (*He gestures at* **Johnstone**.) Do you think he snores?

**Guran** *and* **Akbar** *roar with laughter.* **Nazarine** *playfully hits* **One Eight**.

**Nazarine** (*in Farsi*)  Of course not. He's English.

*More laughter.* **One Eight** *puts the case by the wall.* **Johnstone** *sips his drink.* **Shahin** *comes to the rescue.*

**Shahin**  Please. For James. Today we speak English.

*Silence,* **Johnstone** *looks at his feet, realises no one else is wearing shoes.*

**Johnstone**  Shit. Was I supposed to take my shoes off?


*Exterior: Garden – Day*

**Johnstone**, *a solitary figure, stands unsteadily at the end of a narrow strip of lawn.*

**Guran, Nazarine, One Eight** *and* **Akbar**, *coats draped over their shoulders, wait at the opposite end, silently marvelling at* **Johnstone**. *Along from them,* **Shahin** *stands behind her camera and tripod, focusing a shot.* **Henry**, *notebook in hand, waits for instructions next to her.*

**Henry** (*sotto voce, to* **Shahin**)  You're gonna have to kiss him.

**Shahin** *looks up.* **Henry** *attempts innocence.* **Shahin** *holds out the shutter-release cable.*

**Shahin**  Press this.

**Henry** *takes the cable.* **Shahin** *goes to* **Johnstone**, *takes him by the hand, turns him towards her. Sensing an embrace,* **Johnstone** *discreetly wipes his mouth with the back of his hand. The Iranians, prompted by* **Nazarine**, *look away,* **Johnstone** *leans in, kisses* **Shahin** *chastely on the lips.* **Henry** *takes the shot.*

**Henry** (*consulting notebook*)  OK. Best man.

*No one moves. The Iranians confer in Farsi, put forward* **Guran** *as candidate.*

**Henry** (*to* **Guran**)  You went to wedding?

**Guran** *shrugs.* **One Eight** *nudges him forward.*

**One Eight**  Guran is our very best man. Police don't have his picture.

*He laughs.* **Henry** *calls to* **Johnstone**.

**Henry**  Who give you ring?

**Johnstone**  The black guy.

**Henry**  Raouf? Count your finger, Mr Johnstone. (*To* **Guran**.) You smile? Look happy?

**Guran** *grins, goes to join* **Johnstone**. *The Iranians applaud his debut.* **Shahin** *returns to her camera.*

**Shahin** (*to* **Henry**)  Is that all?

**Henry** *studies her book. The window behind the Iranians opens.* **Mr Kalinowski**, *in his sixties, Polish, peers out as the Iranians move aside.* **Henry** *gives* **Shahin** *a questioning look.*

**Shahin** (*low*)  I forgot.

*Interior:* **Shahin**'s *Flat, Kitchen* – *Day*

*The light is fading, a fitted neon in the kitchen unit lit.* **Johnstone**, *glassy-eyed but alert, his jacket off, sits at the kitchen table, a packet of new pyjamas in his hands. He sips from his milk-shake, peers at the pyjamas. Opposite,* **Shahin** *studies the completed Home Office forms, various documents – birth certificate, registration card, etc. – spread across the table. Behind her, a large pan of rice bubbles on the stove. From the living room, Iranian music, the chatter of the guests.*

**Johnstone** (*finally*)  Not my favourite colour. Blue.

**Shahin** *glances at the pyjamas, returns to the forms.*

**Shahin**  They're new. They must be worn.

**Johnstone** (*scoffs*)  They're not gonna come snooping. They got better things to do. Why can't I sign on?

**Shahin**  You're supposed to have money.

**Johnstone**  Am I?

**Shahin** *ignores him, pushes the forms across the table, holds out a pen.* **Johnstone** *sighs, takes the pen, looks down at the papers, wearying of the detail. Behind him,* **Henry** *slips through the door, waits in the shadows.*

**Johnstone** (*indicating*)  Here?

**Shahin** *nods.* **Johnstone** *goes to sign, hesitates, drops his head, snorts.*

**Johnstone**  God, what have I done?

**Shahin** *shoots an anxious glance at* **Henry**. **Johnstone** *sighs, flourishes* *the pen, signs with exaggerated abandon. He slides the forms across to* **Shahin**, *props his head on his hand.* **Shahin** *checks the signatures, hands* **Johnstone** *an envelope of money.*

**Johnstone** (*taking it*)  You better know what you're doing.

*They look at each other, smile, suddenly amused, the tension released.*

**Shahin**  I hope you will be comfortable in my house.

**Johnstone**  It'll do. Right. Party time.

*He pushes himself to his feet.* **Henry** *opens the door to the living room.* **Johnstone** *salutes her as he passes.*

**Johnstone**  See you at the Karate Club.

*He goes. The guests cheer his arrival.* **Henry** *closes the door.*

**Henry**  Mr Kalinowski wants to kiss you. When he wakes up.

**Shahin** *smiles, puts the forms into an envelope, seals it. She thinks, looks at* **Henry**, *tears in her eyes.*

**Shahin**  Oh Henry. Henry.

*She puts a hand to her mouth, checks the wave of emotion. She picks up the envelope, kisses it, beams at Henry, her eyes wet.*

**Henry**  You wanna eat?

**Shahin** *nods.*


*Interior:* **Shahin**'s *Flat, Living Room – Night*

*Slow pan round the silent faces of the guests.* **Akbar** *smokes,* **Guran** *picks at a plate of food.* **Nazarine**'s *eyes wander round the room,* **Shahin** *stares at the floor as* **Johnstone** *afloat on booze, attacks his second plate of chicken and rice. Beyond him,* **Mr Kalinowski,** *glass in hand, sits with his eyes closed.*

**Johnstone**  I mean you've had a revolution, right? What happened? You kicked out one guy and got another one who reckons he's God or Allah or whatever you call him. . .

**Guran**  Khomeini.

**Johnstone**  Yeah, him. Hey. Your English's not bad. Give that man a banana.

**Akbar** *pats* **Guran** *on the head.* **Guran** *smiles.*

**Johnstone**  So where's it got you? It's a cock-up. You're still stuck, wandering about. Sleeping on floors. Here.

*He passes his plate to* **Shahin**. **Nazarine** *takes it, goes to the kitchen.* **Johnstone** *picks the crumbs from his lap.*

**Johnstone**  There's Iranians in Stevenage. I've seen them. Okay. Iran's bad news and all that. But Stevenage? Forget it. It's a shitheap. I've been in London eighteen months, right. Done the pubs, the discos, met a lot of interesting people. Hundreds. This guy turned up at the squat, few weeks back (*He looks around for his drink.*) Drink. Drink. Hey, I'm really pissed. Where's Prawn Crackers? (**Akbar** *hands him his beaker.*) Oh. Ta. Yeah, hitched from Greece. You know, walked. Gave me a few addresses. Really nice guy. Told him I was planning a trip. Europe, Africa, I don't know. Get a car. Off. (*He turns to* **Shahin**.) You got to. This place'll get you down. Booze and snooker. Sleeping on floors. . .

*The doorbell rings.* **Johnstone** *carries on oblivious.* **Shahin** *gets up, is intercepted by* **Henry** *coming out of the bedroom.*

**Henry**  I've made up bed. You want me put him to sleep?

**Shahin**  What did you put in his drink? (**Henry** *shrugs,* **Shahin** *shakes her head.*) I'll get it.

*Interior: Hall – Night*

**Shahin** *opens the front door.* **Javad** *stands on the step. He takes a small package from behind his back, holds it out to* **Shahin**. **Shahin** *takes it, beckons him in.*

*Interior: Kitchen – Night*

**Shahin** *holds a camera lens in her hand, admires it. The wrapping from the parcel is on the table. In the living room,* **Johnstone**'s *seminar has ended. Music plays.*

**Javad** *leans against the sink, enjoying* **Shahin**'s *obvious pleasure in the gift.*

**Shahin** (*in Farsi*)  Thank you.

**Javad** (*in Farsi*)  It's second-hand. But something you can use.

**Shahin** *packs the lens away.* **Javad** *takes a canister of film from his* *pocket, puts it on the table.*

**Javad** (*in Farsi*) Mina brought it. I thought you might do some prints for us. There's no hurry. Next week'll do.

**Shahin** *glowers at him, not wanting to argue. There is a cheer from the living room.* **Henry** *appears, beckons* **Shahin** *to witness the cause of the merriment.* **Shahin** *turns. From her P.O.V. we see* **Johnstone**, *very drunk, mauling* **Akbar** *in an attempt at a bear-hug.* **Johnstone** *clocks* **Shahin**, *clenches his fist in salute.*

**Johnstone** Vive le France!

*He stumbles, staggers round the furniture, steered by the shouts of the guests, makes it to his room, slams the door.* **Akbar** *turns to the others, mimics* **Johnstone**'s *performance. Everyone laughs.*

**Henry** (*O.O.S.*)  Too much strawberry, eh?

*Interior:* **Shahin**'s *Flat, Bedroom/Living Room – Night*

*Shot of an open wardrobe, a suit hanging among* **Shahin**'s *clothes.* **Shahin**, *in a dressing-gown, her hair loose, adds a second suit to the rack, closes the door. We follow her into the empty living room, all signs of the party gone.*

**Johnstone**'s *tie lies over the back of the sofa, his suitcase on a chair by the wall.* **Shahin** *picks up the tie, rolls it, goes to the case: a jumper, bundles of ties in cellophane packets, socks, a polythene wash-bag, T-shirts, one with a picture of Sydney Opera House on the front. Sticking out from under the clothes, a paperback book, the cover obscured.* **Shahin** *tosses in the tie, lifts the book: a 1984 (i.e. out of date) edition of the Eurail Guide, 'How to Travel Europe and all the World by Train' flashed across the top. She opens the book at a marker, reads. We see the page: A list of travel routes, basic tourist information, currency, places to visit, border regulations. At the top of the page, 'Chapter Ten: IRAN'.*

**Shahin** *drops the book into the case, closes it. She crosses to* **Johnstone**'s *door, listens, opens it a fraction. From her P.O.V. we see* **Johnstone**, *fully clothed, sprawled face down on the bed.* **Shahin** *rests her head against the door, thinks.*

*Exterior: (Dream) – Day*
**Shahin**, *cream jacket, red shoes, runs along the mountain track.*

*Ahead, nearing the summit, the two women approach the* **Man**.
**Shahin** *stumbles, her camera slips from her neck, rolls down the track,
spilling film.* **Shahin** *hurries back, stoops down to retrieve the camera.
Paper money blows from the open purse in her hand. She snatches at it,
gives up, grabs the camera, turns. Ahead, the two women disappear
over the summit, helped by the* **Man**.

*Interior:* **Bamdaad***'s Office, Kensington Market – Day*

*Close up colour photo of the interior of a flat, furnished Iranian style:
rugs, wall hangings, antiques. Underneath, the details written in Farsi.*

**Bamdaad** (*O.O.S., in Farsi*)  No one wants it.

**Shahin** *stands looking at the picture on the office wall.* **Bamdaad**,
*gloomily contemplating another day, sits at his desk, a box of sweetmeats
in his hand. He selects a piece, eats, sighs.*

**Bamdaad** (*in Farsi*)  I offer them beautiful homes. Everything
they want. And what do they do? They go to America.

*He offers* **Shahin** *a sweetmeat from the box.*

**Bamdaad** (*in Farsi*)  A little piece of home.

**Shahin** (*surprised – in Farsi*)  From Iran? Where did you get
them?

*She takes one, eats.* **Bamdaad** *twinkles, conspiratorial.*

**Bamdaad** (*in Farsi*)  I told you. Anything you need. Food,
fabrics, samovar. Come to Bamdaad. (*He gives her the box.*)
Here. Keep it.

**Shahin** (*in Farsi*)  Thank you.

**Bamdaad** *goes to his desk, flips open a file, takes out a list of
addresses, hands it to* **Shahin**. *He spots the wedding ring on her
finger, smiles.*

**Bamdaad** (*in Farsi*)  How's Mr Johnstone?

*Exterior: Street, Kensington – Day*

*Long shot along the secluded street, mansion blocks on either side, a
few parked cars with foreign plates in view.* **Johnstone**, *a pioneer with
no sense of direction, stands in the road scrutinising a turning to the
right. He looks towards us, points, calls to* **Shahin**.

**Johnstone** Down here. Come on.

**Shahin**, *fifty yards behind him, waits by a turning to the left, her camera bag on her shoulder. From her P.O.V., we watch as* **Johnstone** *labours back, hand trying a car door as he approaches. He stops in front of* **Shahin**.

**Johnstone** What?

**Shahin** *nods at the street sign behind him.* **Johnstone** *turns, looks. A beat.*

**Johnstone** You sure you're not Irish?

*He sets off.* **Shahin** *laughs to herself, follows.*


*Interior: Third Floor Flat, Living Room – Day*

**Shahin** *pulls a dust sheet off the sofa, adds it to a pile in the corner. The room has been stripped of personal effects, only basic furniture remains: chairs, table, a bureau.* **Shahin** *goes to her bag, takes out a tripod, begins to assemble it. We hear a sudden crash,* **Johnstone**'s *voice, muffled, remote, cursing.* **Shahin** *stops, turns to the sound.* **Johnstone** *appears, heading for the bedrooms, intent on a thorough search of the flat.* **Shahin** *watches as he passes.*

**Johnstone** (*on the move*) Watch out in the kitchen. Cupboard's a bit dodgy.


*Interior: Third Floor Flat, Entrance Hall – Day*

**Shahin**'s *camera and tripod stand in front of the flat door, angled to take a shot of the corridor and the living room beyond.* **Shahin** *enters the frame, a half chewed apple in her hand, squeezes between the wall and the tripod, makes a fine adjustment to the camera.*

**Johnstone** (*O.O.S.*) Who's he gonna rent it to?

**Shahin** I told you. I don't know.

**Johnstone** (*O.O.S.*) Must cost a fortune.

**Shahin** *ignores him, bites her apple, looks along the line of the shot. She slides the cable release under her thumb, presses. As she does so,* **Johnstone** *steps out of a side room, a Harrods carrier in his hand, right into the middle of the shot.*

**Johnstone** (*flinching*) Oi.

*He grins at* **Shahin. Shahin** *bites her apple, chews, mustering patience.* **Johnstone** *holds up the carrier, produces an empty whisky bottle.*

**Johnstone**  There's a stack of empties in there. Leaving party, I suppose. (*He drops the bottle in the bag.*) Who d'you say's gonna rent it?

**Shahin** *throws the apple at him, hits the wall.* **Johnstone** *ducks, clutching the carrier.* **Shahin** *fires the camera, once, twice, three times.* **Johnstone** *retreats, blinded by the flash.*

**Johnstone**  Get off! What're you doing?

*He disappears into the safety of the living room.* **Shahin** *flicks her hair back, takes a breath.*


*Exterior: Street, Kensington – Day*

**Shahin** *and* **Johnstone** *pick their way through the shoppers.* **Shahin** *has a carrier of groceries,* **Johnstone***, the camera bag.* **Shahin** *unused to public appearances with* **Johnstone***, does her best to look detached.*

**Johnstone**  The people moving into these places are loaded. I'm telling you. You have to know a few.

**Shahin**  You think I marry you if I did?

**Johnstone**  I'm talking about Iranians. There wouldn't be much point you marrying an Iranian, would there. (*Remembering.*) Anyway, you're married.

**Shahin**  Ah yes. I forgot. Stupid Shahin.

**Johnstone**  I just need a couple of contacts. Preferably with an oil well or two but I'll settle for a car. All this coming and going there's bound to be a car going spare. Your lot leave Rollers parked at Heathrow for six months.

**Shahin**  This is Arab.

**Johnstone**  What?

**Shahin**  At Heathrow. Oil-Sheik.

**Johnstone**  That's what I'm saying.

**Shahin**  I am not Arab. And I don't drive.

**Johnstone**  Oh yeah. Cycle to Harrods do you?

**Shahin** *stops, gives* **Johnstone** *the carrier, takes the camera bag.*

**Shahin** I prefer Marks & Spencer. This is Jewish. And I walk. (*She shoulders her bag.*) I don't know every Iranian in London and they don't know me. Until I have a visa, I want to keep it like this. I'm not supposed to be working, remember?

**Johnstone** What you doing it for, then?

**Shahin** I have to pay for you.

*She moves off.* **Johnstone** *watches her go, defeated.*

*Interior: Photo Lab, Kensington – Day*

*Close shot of the counter. A purse, up-ended, spills coins across the surface. A hand enters the frame, slides 10p to one side, hesitates, retreats. Nearby, the buzz and crackle of a short wave radio.*

**Woman's Voice** (*O.O.S.*) Another twenty.

**Shahin** *flustered, clutching her purse, stands by the counter looking blankly at the coins. Opposite, the* **Lab Assistant** *leans on the counter, head propped on her elbows, absorbed in the game. A* **Bike Boy**, *leather suit, helmet, short wave clipped to his chest, stands watching along from* **Shahin**. *The* **Bike Boy** *leans in, teases a 20p from under the remaining copper, flicks it towards the* **Assistant**. *She looks at him wearily.*

**Assistant** Clever clogs. (*To* **Shahin**.) You been feeding the 5,000 or something.

*She hands* **Shahin** *an envelope of processed colour transparencies and two packets of prints, scoops the silver from the counter, goes.* **Shahin** *purses her change, takes the transparencies to the light box by the window, attaches them, flips the switch. Nothing. She sighs, goes to hit it.*

**Bike Boy** (*O.O.S.*) Try hitting it.

**Shahin** (*not turning*) Yes. I know.

*She smacks the side of the box once, twice. The light flickers but refuses to work.* **Shahin** *unclips the transparencies, moves to the window to look at the shots. From* **Shahin**'s *P.O.V. we look down into the mews. The* **Storeman** *kneels on a carpet rolled out in front of the warehouse. An* **Iranian Man**, *grey suit, dark glasses, carrier bags in each hand, stands to one side, inspecting the carpet.*

**Shahin** *holds up the film, scans the shots of the apartments,*
**Johnstone** *visible in several frames. Distracted,* **Shahin** *lowers the*
*film, looks into the mews. We see a* **Mullah***, fully robed, horn-rimmed*
*specs, appears from under the bay door of the warehouse. He advances*
*down the carpet, thumbing his prayer beads, nodding appreciatively.*
*The* **Iranian Man** *looks up at* **Shahin***.*

**Bike Boy** (*O.O.S.*)  Not your day is it.

**Shahin** *turns, looks at him, blank. He smiles.*

**Bike Boy**  I'd go home if I was you.


*Interior:* **Shahin***'s Flat, Living Room – Night*

*Close shot of a photo album open on the table. Above it, a stack of*
*prints of the wedding, one of* **Mr Kalinowski** *and the Iranian guests*
*on top.* **Shahin** *flips through the album, removing pictures of her*
*student days. Over this:*

**Shahin** (*O.O.S.*)  When Shah fell I was already here. There
were parties, demonstrations, meetings – so many meetings. We
didn't know what else to do. We wanted to be there. To see it.

*We see a group of* **Shahin, Jamshid** *and other students, gathered on*
*college steps.* **Shahin** *studies it, puts it face down with other discarded*
*prints.*

**Johnstone**  Why didn't you go?

**Shahin**  I thought about it. Some friends of mine went back. I
decided not to. It's a long story.

**Johnstone** *lies on the sofa, the pyjamas over his jeans and tee-shirt, a*
*peaked cap pushed back on his head. The remains of a meal litter the*
*floor beside him. He watches* **Shahin.**

**Johnstone**  Anyone special?

**Shahin** (*not listening*)  Mmm?

**Johnstone**  Your friends.

*He nods at the picture in her hand: a shot of* **Shahin** *and* **Jamshid.**
**Shahin** *shakes her head, puts the picture down.*

**Shahin**  My parents. You enjoy your meal?

**Johnstone**  Yeah. What was it?

**Shahin** Ghormehsabzy. Very beautiful Persian dish. I'll teach you how to make it.

**Johnstone** *fiddles with his cap, thinks.*

**Johnstone** I'd've gone back.

**Shahin** (*smiles*) I don't think so.

**Johnstone** I would. Things like that don't happen here. I mean, can you imagine a million people marching up to Buckingham Palace and telling the Queen to piss off? Forget it. They'd all just stand there waving daffodils and singing songs. (*He looks across at* **Shahin**.) It's a flower. You know. Like a tulip. (**Shahin** *nods.*) Makes you sick. As for the church taking over, it'd be a bishop, I suppose. Archbishop of Canterbury. I can't see anyone being scared shitless of him. Unless he started pulling fingernails. Not that kinda bloke. Loves cats. (*He looks at* **Shahin**.) Got you though, hasn't he. Khomeini. Up here.

*He taps his forehead.* **Shahin** *stands, starts to clear the table.*

**Shahin** Let's not talk about this. It's late.

**Johnstone** See what I mean? Mention the guy's name, the room goes quiet.

*He swings off the sofa, crosses to the table, starts to unbutton his jacket.*

**Shahin** It's boring. For me. There is more to life than politics. Iran is not just Khomeini. We have poets, singers, beautiful things.

**Johnstone** *reaches for the discarded prints, curious.* **Shahin** *gets to them first, slips them inside the cover of the album.*

**Shahin** If you want politics, then go to Iran. Here, it's a game. All they do is fight each other, blame each other. And it's dangerous. English people don't want to see this. We are guests here.

**Johnstone** *pulls the cord on his pyjamas.* **Shahin**, *album clutched to her chest, doesn't know where to look.*

**Johnstone** It's all right. I've got me clothes on.

**Shahin** *moves past, goes into her bedroom.* **Johnstone** *takes off the pyjamas, his back to the door.*

**Johnstone** I signed one of those petitions the other day.

Against the tortures and that. Tottenham Court Road. They'd never heard of you.

**Shahin** *appears in the doorway, concerned.*

**Shahin** You gave address?

**Johnstone** Well, every little helps. (*He gives* **Shahin** *the pyjamas.*) You gonna put them under your pillow?

**Shahin** I have to sleep.

*She goes, closes the door.* **Johnstone** *waits, thinks.*


*Interior:* **Shahin**'*s Bedroom — Night*

*Shot of* **Shahin**'*s worktable, the curtain drawn, the anglepoise lit. On the table, a small bundle of letters in Farsi script. The bundle has been opened, one or two letters read.*

**Shahin** *drops into the shot, sits at the table. She wears her dressing gown, her hair loose. She looks down at the letters, thinks. She stands, crosses to the wardrobe, opens it, racks through the clothes. She finds her wedding suit, takes it out, fishes in the pockets. She takes something from the side pocket. We see it is* **Mina**'*s canister of film.*

**Shahin** *sits on the bed, turns the canister over in her hands.*


*Interior: Basement Storeroom, Chelsea College — Day*

*Shot of delivery chute on a battered duplicator, a sheaf of Farsi leaflets piling up in the tray. The machine clanks and whirrs, approaching yet another breakdown. A hand grabs a leaflet.*

**Nick** (*O.O.S.*) That's better. Keep praying.

**Nick** *stands by the duplicator, discarded paper at his feet, examining the leaflet. Alongside,* **Akbar**, *sleeves rolled, hands covered in ink, gently strokes the machine, muttering in Farsi as he gently winds the drum.* **Shahin**, *uneasy, bag at her feet, waits by the door of the cramped room. Across from her, the* **Student** *sits on packets of paper putting the finishing touches to a cardboard fez.*

**Akbar** (*to* **Nick**) Show it to Shahin.

**Nick** *hands* **Shahin** *the leaflet. She glances at it, eyes* **Akbar**, *anxious to talk. Finally, she reaches into her bag.*

**Shahin** I can't wait —

**Akbar** *shushes her, intent on his work.* **Shahin** *stiffens a little. The machine jams, the metal housing clatters to the floor.*

**Akbar** Shit.

*The* **Student** *gives* **Shahin** *a weary look, turns to* **Nick.**

**Student** Told you comrade. Sabotage.

**Akbar** (*to* Nick) You know who does this? Every night they come and break it. Fucking terrorists.

**Student** Iraqis.

**Akbar** Israeli. This college full of Israeli.

**Nick** *picks up the housing, looks at it.*

**Nick** Probably the Labour Party. They got a fetish about paper.

*The door is knocked. A beat.* **Akbar**, *the* **Student** *and* **Nick** *quickly gather up the printed material. The* **Student** *peels the stencil from the duplicator.* **Akbar** *goes to* **Shahin**, *takes the leaflet from her hand, adds it to the bundle in his arms.*

**Shahin** It's good.

**Akbar** It's shit. I'm a peasant Shahin. We need an artist.

*He moves out, beckons* **Shahin** *to follow.* **Nick** *holds open the door for her.* **Shahin** *takes her bag, goes.*

*Interior: Chelsea College, Corridor – Day*

*Groups of* **Students**, *mainly overseas, pass along the corridor, heading for classes.* **Akbar**, **Shahin** *and* **Nick** *move towards us,* **Akbar** *handing copies of the leaflet to one or two* **Iranians** *as he goes.*

**Nick** (*to* Akbar) Give me some for the poly.

**Akbar** Do the bar. (*He gives* **Nick** *a bundle.*) Iranian intellectual love this place.

**Shahin** *stops. Ahead, from her P.O.V., we see* **Johnstone** *through the glass partition of the coffee bar.* **Shahin** *puts her hand on* **Akbar**'s *arm.*

**Shahin** Take these. I have to go.

*She gives* **Akbar** *a large envelope from her bag.* **Akbar** *gives* **Nick** *his* *bundle, pulls out the prints, skims through.* **Shahin** *moves in protectively, concealing the pictures from passers-by, her back to* **Johnstone. Akbar** *picks out a picture of* **Mina,** *in combat gear, shows it to* **Nick.**

**Nick** Mina?

**Akbar** (*nods – to* **Shahin**) Beautiful. Thank you.

*Two* **Iranian Students** *walk past.* **Nick** *gives the* **First Student** *a leaflet.* **Akbar** *tries to intercept it, misses. The* **First Student** *pushes him off,* **Akbar** *flattens him against the wall with one hand, takes the leaflet with the other. The* **Second Student** *opts for disdain.*

**Akbar** (*to* **First Student**, *in Farsi*) Only when you've learnt to read, my friend.

**Akbar** *turns to* **Nick** *and* **Shahin**, *takes his bundle. Behind him, the* **Students** *go, ruffled but cool.*

**Akbar** (*to* **Nick**) Don't try to change the world in one day. You'll have nothing to do tomorrow. Every Iranian is not like Mina. (*He pats him on the back.*) The poly, eh?

**Nick** *sheepishly trudges off.*

**Akbar** (*to* **Shahin**) Will you come?

**Shahin** No.

**Akbar** (*a glance at the prints*) So why. . . ?

**Johnstone** (*O.O.S.*) Hey, Akbar. . .

**Akbar** *and* **Shahin** *turn.* **Johnstone**, *in combat fatigues, moves briskly up towards them.*

**Akbar** (*expansive*) Mr Johnstone. You come to beat me for stealing your wife? (*He hands him some leaflets.*) Here. Give some to your friends. There's food, dancing.

**Johnstone** *studies the leaflet.* **Shahin** *scoffs.*

**Shahin** (*to* **Johnstone**) This is not for you. Everything will be in Farsi.

**Akbar** He can eat in English.

**Shahin** (*fast, in Farsi*) I don't want him to go.

**Akbar** (*in Farsi*) There's no harm.

**Shahin** (*in Farsi*)  I said no.

**Akbar** *backs off, gives* **Johnstone** *a shrug.* **Johnstone** *looks at* **Shahin***, puzzled.*

**Shahin**  Come. Let's go.

*She sets off.* **Akbar** *looks at* **Johnstone***'s outfit.*

**Akbar**  New?

**Johnstone**  Fancied a change. (*He fingers his ear.*) You know anyone with a car? I wanna –

**Akbar** (*not listening*)  She won't like it.

*He nods towards* **Shahin***.* **Johnstone** *turns, sees* **Shahin** *making for the exit.*

**Johnstone** (*to* **Shahin**)  Hang on. (*He turns back to* **Akbar***.*) I'll bring. . .

**Akbar** *has gone.* **Johnstone** *sighs.*

*Exterior: Street – Day*

*A* **Girl***, in her twenties, tanned, dark hair, a rucksack on her back, several jumpers tied round her waist, hurries towards us, a quizzical smile on her face. Beyond her, an* **Arab Man***, in his sixties, white shift, squats on a mattress at the door to his ground floor flat, contemplating the world.*

**Johnstone** (*O.O.S.*)  Shit. Don't say anything.

**Shahin** *and* **Johnstone** *stand outside an Arab newsagents, Middle East dailies on display, heading for an apartment block across the street. The* **Girl** *slows, greets* **Johnstone, Shahin** *dropping back, keeping her distance.*

**Girl** (*Australian accent*)  Hi. Fancy seeing you, you little wanker. (*She slips an arm out of her pack.*) Give us a hand. (**Johnstone** *eases the pack to the ground.*) Christ, I stink. I could really use a bath. I just got back from Spain. And my period's just started. What're you doing here?

**Johnstone** (*flustered, turning to* **Shahin**)  This is a friend of mine, Shahin.

**Girl**  Come again?

**Johnstone** Shahin.

**Girl** (*to* **Shahin**) You're not Spanish are you? Sorry. That place is the pits. (*To* **Johnstone**.) Where's she from?

**Johnstone** (*to* **Shahin**) Where you from?

**Shahin** Iran.

*The* **Girl** *raises her eyebrows.* **Johnstone**, *edgy, glances at the traffic.*

**Girl** (*to* **Johnstone**) Wanna come for a beer or something? Bring your friend.

**Johnstone** (*moving*) No, we gotta go. I'll catch you later.

*He darts across the street, narrowly missed by a passing car that blares its horn, disappears into the courtyard of the apartment block. The* **Girl**, *nonplussed, watches.*

**Girl** Well, fuck you. What a creep. (**Shahin** *makes to cross the street.*) He asked you to marry him yet?

**Shahin** *stops, looks at the* **Girl**. *The* **Girl** *scoffs, shoulders her sack, stomps off.*

*Interior: First Floor Apartment, Living Room – Day*

*The furniture has been pushed into one corner, a trestle table set up in the centre of the room. Decorators' equipment – paint, wallpaper rolls, brushes, tools – stacked against the wall by the window. The work is obviously incomplete, one wall stripped to the plaster.*

**Shahin**, *her camera bag at her feet, stands looking at the room. She sighs, takes the list of addresses from her bag, studies it.* **Johnstone** *calls from the bottom.*

**Johnstone** (*O.O.S.*) Hey. Have a look at this.

*Interior: First Floor Apartment, Bathroom – Day*

**Johnstone** *leans against the washbasin, a Farsi leaflet in his hand, looking at the toilet. A carpeted rostrum, new, has been fitted round the base converting it to an Islamic squatting toilet. The packaging lies to one side.*

*The toilet roll dispenser, unscrewed from the wall, sits on the washbasin surround, the paper spilling into the basin.*

**Johnstone** You sure you got the right address? Looks like he's expecting someone special. (*He hands her the leaflet.*) What's it say?

**Shahin** (*reading*) They're instructions.

**Johnstone** *waits for more.* **Shahin**, *uneasy, folds the leaflet, slips it in her pocket.*

**Shahin** (*dismissive*) It's a custom.

**Johnstone** You haven't got one.

**Shahin** No. (*She looks at the toilet a moment, turns.*) Who was the girl?

**Johnstone** Stayed at the squat. Know what? I reckon it's the Embassy plumbers. Gonna bug the flat. Bamdaad said they keep tabs on people. There'll be a few deals done in a place like this. The whole block's –

**Shahin** *suddenly wheels round, flashes with anger.*

**Shahin** Stop it. These stupid questions. All the time.

**Johnstone** *freezes, taken aback.* **Shahin** *looks down, calms herself.*

**Shahin** I'm sorry.

**Johnstone** *slowly gathers himself, finds resentment.*

**Johnstone** What's got into you?

**Shahin** *goes to him, puts a hand on his arm.*

**Shahin** (*quiet, serious*) When my money was stopped – sometimes they do this because they think you are against them. To make you go back. (*She looks down, choosing her words carefully.*) I have family in Iran, friends. If they think I'm involved in – (*She stops, swallows.*) If they think –

*She stops again, dealing with an unexpected fear. Tears well up in her eyes.* **Johnstone** *watches, puzzled.*

**Johnstone** What is it?

**Shahin** *takes a breath, shakes her head.*

**Shahin** It's nothing. I don't sleep. (*She rubs her eyes.*) The community here is very small. People talk. You mustn't tell anyone what I do. Or where I go. (*She searches his face for reassurance.*) I don't know why this has happened to me.

Someone must have said bad things. We must be careful.

**Johnstone** (*finally*)  OK. Mum's the word.

**Shahin** *smiles her gratitude, studies the room a moment.*

**Shahin** (*moving*)  This is wrong place. I'd better see Bamdaad.

*She goes.* **Johnstone** *calls after her.*

**Johnstone**  Hey, don't be late.

*The door bangs.* **Johnstone** *sighs, turns to the mirror, admires himself.*

**Johnstone**  Knees up with the comrades.


*Interior: Kensington Market – Day*

*Long shot of the corridor outside* **Bamdaad**'s *office.* **Bamdaad** *emerges from his office, talking to an unseen customer. He waits, composed, deferrent. Finally, the* **Iranian Man** *leads* **Bamdaad** *away, a hand on his back.*

**Shahin** *continues towards the office, looks in through the window. We see the picture of the* **Shah** *has been removed from the wall.*


*Interior:* **Shahin**'s *Flat, Bathroom – Night*

*Shot of the bath, the taps running, the bath filling with water.* **Shahin** *sits on the toilet, thinking. On the floor,* **Johnstone**'s *socks and pants, a pair of scruffy trainers.* **Shahin** *stands, puts the socks and pants in a washing basket, turns off the taps. She makes a decision, pulls out the bath plug, goes.*


*Interior:* **Shahin**'s *Flat, Living Room – Night*

**Shahin**, *struggling into her coat, opens the flat door.* **Mr Kalinowski**, *in tatty flannels and slippers, stands there, a light bulb in his hand.* **Shahin** *jumps, puts a hand to her chest.*

**Kalinowski**  Is Mr Johnstone there?

**Shahin**  No, he's not.

**Kalinowski** *shakes his head, irritated.*

**Kalinowski**  I have no light.

*Interior:* **Kalinowski**'s *Flat – Night*

*Streetlight through open curtains. In the corner, a bird-cage hangs from a stand, glinting in the gloom. The budgie sits on top of the cage, chirping.*

**Shahin** *stands waiting for* **Kalinowski** *in the centre of the room, under the light.* **Kalinowski** *has gone to fetch a chair. He calls.*

**Kalinowski** Two days now, I go to bed early.

*The budgie flies round the room, settles on* **Shahin**'s *head.* **Shahin** *is startled but stays still.* **Kalinowski** *emerges from his bedroom carrying a chair.*

**Shahin** You have a friend.

**Kalinowski** (*breathless*) Today I am not tired. (*He positions the chair under the light, sees the budgie.*) What are you doing. Stupid thing. (*He flaps his hand at the budgie, it flies back to the cage.*) Can you reach?

**Shahin** *tests the chair: it wobbles.*

**Shahin** It's not very safe.

**Kalinowski** I'll hold it.

*He gestures for* **Shahin** *to get onto the chair, holds the back.* **Shahin** *climbs up, reaches for the old bulb.*

**Kalinowski** (*looking up*) You marry Mr Johnstone for your visa?

*The chair wobbles.* **Shahin** *gives a start.* **Kalinowski** *puts a hand on her hip.*

**Kalinowski** I've got you.

**Shahin** *fumbles out the old bulb.*

**Shahin** He's my husband. He was away. It wasn't easy. . . (*She hands him the old bulb.*) . . . to see each other.

**Kalinowski** (*smiles*) I understand.

*He hands her the new bulb.* **Shahin**, *trembling, takes it, reaches up.* **Kalinowski** *puts both hands on her hips, edges his shoulder against her legs. The budgie flies round the room, circling the couple.* **Shahin** *puts in the bulb.*

**Shahin** Please. Let me down.

**Kalinowski** (*helping her off the chair*) Your hand is shaking. Are you all right?

**Shahin** (*hand on chest*) I'm fine. Thank you.

*She makes for the door.* **Kalinowski** *flips on the light, puts a hand on her arm.*

**Kalinowski** One moment. (*He studies her face.*) The English, you know. These people have ruled the world. And they know nothing. You are safe here.

**Shahin** *removes his hand, goes.*


*Exterior: Side of Street near Church Hall – Night*

*Shot of the entrance to the hall, Iranian music heard through the open doors. Across the street, a* **Policeman** *leans against the wing of a patrol car. A* **Second Policeman** *sits in the driver's seat, the window down, a newspaper propped against the wheel. On the hall steps, a heated exchange between an* **Iranian Steward** *and two* **Iranian Men** *ends as the men walk off in disgust.*

**Shahin** *hesitates at the foot of the steps, moves as the* **Men** *come towards her in an angry conference. She glances at the patrol car, slips into the hall unnoticed.*


*Interior: Church Hall – Night*

*On a lit stage at the end of the hall, a Kurdish* **Folk Band** *and* **Dancers** *in traditional costume. The dance is reaching a climax, stray figures from the audience joining in at the foot of the stage. In the darkened hall the Iranian and Kurdish audience clap and wave white handkerchiefs in time with the music. We see* **One Eight** *and* **Nazarine** *among the faces.*

**Shahin** *sits alone in the corner of the empty gallery, watching the dance. Two* **Boys**, *one in costume, appear on the far side of the gallery. The* **First Boy** *gives chase to the* **Second**. *They weave between rows of empty chairs, laughing.* **Shahin** *watches. The* **Second Boy** (*in costume*) *runs into her, freezes. The* **First Boy**, *keeping his distance, laughs. Downstairs, the audience burst into applause as the dance ends.*

*The* **Boys** *scurry off. We hear an announcement from the stage.*

**Iranian Man** (*P.A. accoustic; slow*) Ladies and gentlemen. There are some not Iranian here. So there is speeches in English. . .

*Some applause over the murmur of the audience.* **Shahin** *prepares to leave as the house lights come on, looks over the balcony searching for* **Johnstone***. She spots him in the aisle, a pitta bread kebab in hand, scanning faces as he moves towards the exit.*

*Interior: Church Hall Foyer – Night*

**Shahin** *moves down the stairs into the foyer. Posters, flags, trestle tables laden with political literature lend the space a temporary colour.* **Shahin** *catches* **Johnstone***'s eye as he emerges from the hall gnawing his kebab. He comes across, joins her by a display of Kurdish photographs – village scenes, guerrillas, children playing – assembled at the foot of the stairs.*

**Johnstone**  I can't find Akbar.

**Shahin** (*casual*)  I expect he's gone.

**Johnstone**  The other guy's here. The bloke with the cab. (*He nods at the display.*) You didn't say you'd done those. Any of them your friends?

**Shahin** (*a glance*)  It was a long time ago. (*She sees a few people moving out of the hall.*) Come outside.

*She slips out of the door.* **Johnstone** *groans, follows.*

*Exterior: Church Hall Steps – Night*

*Across the road, the* **Second Policeman** *sits in the patrol car. The* **First** *has gone.*

**Johnstone**  What now?

**Shahin**  I want to go home.

**Johnstone**  You only just got here.

**Shahin**  Mr Kalinowski knows. We have to talk.

**Johnstone**  OK. Fire away.

**Shahin** (*looking at the policeman*)  Not here.

**Johnstone** (*realising*)  It's a policeman. We have them over here. They help old ladies cross the road.

*He hurries down the steps.* **Shahin** *pulls her coat round her, follows.*

*Exterior: Side Street, Kensington — Night*

**Shahin** and **Johnstone** *walk by the perimeter wall of the church hall. The wall is spray-canned with Farsi slogans, old posters for assorted events — mystic gurus to political rallies — torn and disfigured by rival factions and bored kids.* **Johnstone**, *annoyed, a pace or two behind* **Shahin**, *idly tries car doors as he discharges his frustration.*

**Johnstone**  You're beginning to cramp my style.

**Shahin** (*not turning*)  I don't know this.

**Johnstone**  What?

**Shahin**  This word. Cramp. What does it mean? I don't know.

**Johnstone**  Cramp? Christ you're thick when you want to be. (*He tries a car.*) Anywhere else you fancy leaving tonight? There's a pub up the road with swing doors. You could be outta there in seconds. (*He moves alongside* **Shahin**.) What I'm saying is, I don't like being told what to do.

**Shahin** *stops, looks at him.*

**Shahin**  You can do what you like. But you don't mix with Iranian. This is not for you.

**Johnstone**  I'm interested that's all. I've got an enquiring mind. It's a very English habit.

*He pulls on a car door. The car alarm goes off, a high pitched wail.*

**Johnstone**  Shit. Come on.

*He runs, turns into the lane running down the back of the hall.* **Shahin** *follows. As she turns the corner, we see a group of men from the hall confronting a rival faction banned from the festivities. A few of the men are in costume, a bare chested* **Caliph** *prominent amongst the group, prepared for the play scheduled to end the evening. Fists are flying, the* **Caliph** *has one of the faction in a head lock; a man in kurdish dress furiously tugs at a flag held by two of the faction. We recognise the two Iranian men in the mêlée.*

**Johnstone** *stands gawping at the sight.* **Shahin**, *breathing hard, looks back up the street. The patrol car, alerted by the alarm, turns the corner, headlamps lit, glides towards the car.* **Shahin** *looks back into the lane.* **Johnstone** *is punched by the faction leader, reels backwards, collides with the* **Caliph**, *is punched by the man in kurdish dress, falls flat on his face.*

*Suddenly, the* **Caliph** *hears the alarm. The fight stops. One of the faction sees* **Shahin**, *starts to run. Both sides rapidly disperse, the men slipping into the backyard of the hall through a wooden gate, the faction tearing off down the lane.* **Johnstone**, *on hands and knees, crawls towards the gate.* **Shahin** *hurries to him, props him against the wall.*

**Shahin**  Are you all right?

**Johnstone** (*feeling his face*)  Yeah.

**Shahin** *examines his face. A man in a Mullah's robe, a Khomeini mask over his face, puts his head round the gate.* **Shahin** *jumps. The man lifts his mask: it's* **Akbar**, *breathless, sweating.*

**Akbar** (*in Farsi*)  What are you . . . (*He sees* **Johnstone**.) Bring him inside.

*He stoops to help* **Johnstone** *to his feet.*

**Shahin** (*in Farsi*)  Leave it. Go.

**Akbar** *disappears. The car alarm stops.* **Shahin** *goes to the corner, looks up the street. The* **Policeman** *ambles round the car giving it a routine check.* **Shahin** *turns back into the lane. Through the wooden gate, she sees the back door of the hall open. Music spills out as the last of the men go inside.* **Shahin** *leans against the wall, waits.*

**Johnstone**  I knew Akbar was around.

*Interior: Chicken Bar, Kitchen Area — Night*

**Johnstone**, *nose grazed, a cut on his cheek, sits on a stool at the back of the kitchen.* **Henry** *cleans him up, First Aid box on the table.* **Shahin** *stands watching by the freezer. In the bar, assorted nomads eat, rest up, ready for the long haul through the night.*

**Henry** (*to* **Shahin**)  How long you been married? You're crazy, Shahin. Stay at home. I don't want dead soldier in kitchen. (*She dries the cut with a kitchen towel. To* **Johnstone**.) Why you dressed like this? You think you in Lebanon?

**Johnstone**  You got a mirror?

**Henry**  Not for this face.

**Johnstone** *gets up — she pushes him back.*

**Henry**  Sit.

*She takes a plaster from the box, peels off the back.*

**Johnstone** (*insistent*) They were trying to bust up the meeting. If I hadn't been there someone could've got hurt. (*To* **Shahin**.) You must know who they were.

**Shahin** I told you. No.

**Johnstone** I give up. One minute half the Arab world's trying to stop you studying then suddenly it's not worth talking about. (**Shahin** *gives him a deadly look.*) Yeah, yeah. I know. Iranians aren't Arabs. There's fifty-seven varieties and none of them's got a car.

**Henry** (*brandishing the plaster*) You wan' this over your mouth?

**Johnstone** Someone's saying bad things about her. She told me. It just crossed my mind it might be one of the whirling dervishes who did this.

*He points to the cut.* **Henry** *applies the plaster.*

**Henry** Mr Johnstone. Let me tell you something. We foreigners fight each other all the time. You know why we do this? 'Cos you English fuck us up.

*She presses the plaster with her thumb.* **Johnstone** *winces.*

**Johnstone** Ow! That hurt.

**Henry** Pleasure

*She holds out her hand.*

**Johnstone** (*blank*) What?

**Henry** You wanna go private, you gotta pay.

**Johnstone**, *uneasy, looks to* **Shahin** *for guidance.*

**Shahin** (*a gesture*) I have no money.

**Johnstone** (*reaching for his pocket*) How much d'you want. . .

**Henry**, *laughs, claps her hands, delighted with the joke.* **Shahin** *joins in, despite herself.* **Johnstone**, *got at, attempts a recovery.*

**Johnstone** No, fair enough. I mean I don't work here.

**Raouf**, *in cinema gear, leans round the corner, a box under each arm, stays the laughter.*

**Raouf** Don't tell me there ain't a God in heaven. Boss man is sick. I never worked so hard in my life.

*He throws* **Henry** *a chocolate bar from the box, disappears.* **Henry** *examines it, makes a face, puts it in* **Johnstone***'s shirt pocket.*

**Henry** Here soldier. Get lost.

*She goes after* **Raouf. Johnstone***, relieved, gets up, inspects his face in the freezer door next to* **Shahin.**

**Johnstone** She's got a fucking weird sense of humour. Come on. I need a drink.

*He beckons* **Shahin** *to follow, sets off through the bar.*

**Shahin** (*not moving*) You go.

**Johnstone** *stops, considers a reply, changes his mind, moves off fast.*

*Exterior: Rear of Chicken Bar — Night*

**Henry** *sits on the wall, looking along the alley. In the distance, the roar of traffic; nearer, a medley of kitchen noise: crates being shifted, dishes washed, rubbish dumped.* **Shahin** *comes out the back door, sits next to* **Henry.**

**Henry** Raouf got a box of shirts in there. You ever buy shirt in cinema?

**Shahin** *smiles, fond.*

**Shahin** Thanks for. . .

**Henry** *waves dismissively, tilts her head back, yawns. A small silence, the two women worn out by the long day.*

**Henry** (*finally*) You wanna divorce?

**Shahin** (*thinking it through*) He's so strange. He follows me everywhere. Everything he does is such a mess. His clothes, his hair. And questions. All the time he asks questions.

**Henry** He's a man. How's the job?

**Shahin** (*frowns*) I don't know.

**Henry** *puts her arm round her.*

**Henry** Shahin. Are you complaining again?

**Shahin** (*laughs*) Yes.

**Henry** I give you something to complain about. (*She pulls her towards the door.*) Raouf's chicken.

*Interior:* **Shahin**'s *Flat, Living Room – Night*

*The table, laid for dinner, two lit candles at either end, has been pulled into the middle of the room.* **Johnstone**'s *ties, knotted to pieces of string, hang over the table like Christmas decorations.*

**Shahin** *stands by the door, taking in the scene.* **Johnstone** *calls from the kitchen.*

**Johnstone** (*O.O.S.*) This is nearly ready.

*The bathroom door opens. The Australian* **Girl** *from the street pads out, towelling her hair. She wears* **Shahin**'s *dressing gown.*

**Girl** Oh hi. I borrowed your stuff. You should've seen the water. Was I dirty.

*She makes a face, heads for* **Johnstone**'s *room.* **Johnstone** *appears from the kitchen, a collander of spaghetti in his hand.*

**Johnstone** Where you been?

**Shahin** Why is she here?

**Girl** Sorry. I'm Ellen. Jimmy said I could use the spare room for the night. I'm heading north tomorrow.

**Johnstone** (*innocent*) You don't mind, do you?

**Shahin** *moves across towards her bedroom.*

**Ellen** Listen, I think it's great you two guys are married. (**Shahin** *looks at her.*) Sounds like you could use some protection round here.

*Interior:* **Shahin**'s *Flat, Living Room – Night*

**Shahin, Johnstone** *and* **Ellen** *sit round the candlelit table.*

**Shahin** *sits patiently listening to* **Ellen**'s *travels.* **Johnstone**, *drunk, fiddles nervously with a tie. The remains of the meal litter the table.* **Shahin** *has not eaten.* **Ellen** *and* **Johnstone** *have wine.*

**Ellen** I stopped off in Japan. It's really pretty. You should go sometime. Food isn't much but they have beautiful mountains.

Funny, you expect everything to be really small. . .

**Johnstone** *snorts with laughter.*

**Ellen**  Hey piss off. She's interested.

**Shahin** *gives a faint smile.* **Johnstone** *puts his head in his hands.*

**Ellen**  I dunno. On a bad day I think – why am I doing all this? I could be home in my own bed. I've been in fifteen different countries since September. Crazy really. I sometimes dream of finding a little place by a river, settling down. . .

**Johnstone** *gets up, giggling, goes into the kitchen.* **Shahin** *watches.*

**Ellen**  Shit Jimmy. You couldn't find your way to the bathroom.

**Johnstone** *comes out of the kitchen, heads straight for* **Shahin**'s *room.*

**Johnstone**  I'm going to bed.

*He goes in, closes the door.* **Shahin** *looks at the table, angry, trying not to show it.*

**Ellen**  Really pisses me off when people do that. (*She sees* **Shahin**'s *expression.*) Hey, I'm not keeping you up am I?

**Shahin**  No. I'll make some tea.

**Ellen** (*rising*) Let me. No milk, lots of sugar, right? (*She goes to the kitchen – calls.*) Tell me about Iran.

**Shahin** *twists her wedding ring.*

*Interior:* **Shahin**'s *Bedroom – Night*

**Johnstone** *lies flat out on* **Shahin**'s *bed, eyes closed. We hear the flush in the bathroom,* **Ellen** *bidding* **Shahin** *goodnight, a door closes.* **Johnstone** *opens his eyes, listens, closes them.*

**Shahin** *comes into the bedroom, looks down at* **Johnstone**, *face tight with anger.* **Johnstone** *peers at her through half-closed eyes.*

**Johnstone**  Hoch and himmel Fritz, it's a woman.

**Shahin** (*quiet, contained*) Get out.

**Johnstone**  What?

**Shahin**  Get out.

**Johnstone** *sits up on his elbows, blinks.*

**Johnstone** Where am I gonna sleep?

**Shahin** You can sleep on sofa.

**Johnstone** But I told her – you know. (*He frowns.*) The sofa? I'll never make it. The buses aren't running.

**Shahin** *goes to the wardrobe, pulls open the bottom drawer, takes out a blanket.* **Johnstone** *slumps back on the bed.*

**Johnstone** (*mumbles*) I could call a cab I suppose.

**Shahin** *throws the blanket at* **Johnstone**. *He doesn't move.* **Shahin** *waits.* **Johnstone** *rolls over onto his side, sighs, his back to* **Shahin**. **Shahin** *grabs hold of his arm, intending to pull him off the bed.* **Johnstone** *swings round, fully awake, pulls* **Shahin** *on top of him.*

**Shahin** (*in Farsi*) Get your hands off me. Get off. . .

*They struggle, the duvet slipping under them, the pillows falling to the floor.* **Johnstone** *laughs, surprised by* **Shahin**'s *strength.* **Shahin** *pulls at his hair.* **Johnstone** *yelps, releases his grip.* **Shahin** *knees him in the groin.* **Johnstone** *rears up in agony, tumbles onto the floor.* **Shahin**, *wide-eyed, breathing hard, stifles a convulsive sob, her fist pressed against her mouth.*

**Johnstone** (*O.O.S., moans*) What you do that for. . . ?

**Shahin** *gets off the bed.* **Johnstone** *slowly gets to his feet. They face each other across the bed.*

**Johnstone** English custom. Home pissed. Play with wife. (*He looks at a smear of blood on his hand.*) I've lost my earring. . .

*He stumbles out.* **Shahin** *quickly goes to her coat on the wardrobe door, takes the key from the pocket, locks the door.*

*Interior:* **Shahin**'s *Bedroom – Night*

**Shahin** *lies in bed, her back towards us. Over this we hear* **Johnstone**, *through the wall, arguing with* **Ellen**. **Shahin** *rolls over. We see she is awake. We hear* **Ellen** *expelling* **Johnstone**, *the bedroom door slam. Silence.* **Shahin** *gets up, takes the pair of pyjamas from under the pillow, puts them in a drawer. She sits on the end of the bed, thinks.*

*Exterior: (Dream) – Day*

**Shahin** *climbs the hill, her camera round her neck, a British passport in her hand. The* **Man** *stands at the top, facing the sun. There is a sudden flapping sound. A flock of birds swoop down the hillside.* **Shahin** *puts up a protective hand, the birds hover, vanish.* **Shahin** *looks at her hand. Blood trickles from her wedding ring. She starts to run, breathing fast. We hear the sound of the Azaan.*

*Exterior: Kensington Gardens – Day*

*A party of Greek tourists, enthusiasm for day five of their off-season package visibly muted, stand gazing at the Serpentine wondering why it is in their guide book. A middle-aged woman sits with her husband dreaming of the sun; their son-in-law identifies the ducks for their daughter.*

**Johnstone** (*O.O.S.*)  Listen. About last night.

**Shahin** *and* **Johnstone** *sit on the terrace of the lakeside café along from the Greeks.* **Johnstone** *has tea and a Danish pastry.* **Shahin** *looks out across the lake, her camera bag at her feet.*

**Shahin**  You were drunk.

**Johnstone** *picks a currant off his pastry, studies her remoteness.*

**Johnstone**  I didn't think it would be like this. Living in the same place. Having you around. It's not easy. (*He chews the currant – casual.*) I fancy you.

**Shahin**  Let's not talk about it.

**Johnstone** *sits back, irritated, fixes on a passing waiter.*

**Johnstone**  Hey. (*The* **Waiter** *stops, tray poised.*) You got any toast? This thing's covered in glue.

**Waiter**  You don't want it?

**Johnstone**  No. I want some toast. You know. Coupla slices, under the grill. Bit of the butter, bit of marmalade. (*The* **Waiter** *shrugs.*) You don't do toast? OK. Where you from? France, right? I walk into a café in Paris, ask for breakfast, what do I get?

**Waiter** (*deadpan*)  What you ordered?

*He glides off, unruffled.* **Johnstone** *shouts after him.*

**Johnstone** Croissant. Think about it.

*He picks up the Danish, throws it into the lake. The Greeks watch, grateful for the distraction.*

**Johnstone** Smart arse. (*He looks at* **Shahin**.) We doing these pictures or what?

**Shahin** (*frowns*) I don't know.

**Johnstone** Oh. Packing it in, are you? I'm not surprised. Takes you all morning to load a camera. That mean I can sign on or do I have to clear it with the Special Branch? (**Shahin** *looks at him – ice.*) I'm only asking.

**Shahin** I'm worried. About Bamdaad.

*She takes the Farsi leaflet from her pocket, looks at it.*

**Shahin** The changes he makes to this flat. These are not for his people. I don't know why he does this.

**Johnstone** Thought you went to see him?

**Shahin** He wasn't there.

**Johnstone** I don't get you. I've lived with you two weeks. No one's called. You won't let me meet your friends. I don't even know if you've got any friends. Okay. You lost your grant. You're getting a visa. Beats me why you wanna stay here.

**Shahin** I want to work. I want to wear what I like. I want to choose who I spend my time with. You think we could do this in Iran? Sit in coffee house, make joke about police? You sign petition but you don't read it.

**Johnstone** (*humbled*) I didn't mean. . . (*He considers a moment.*) If Bamdaad's a problem, let's check it out.

**Shahin** You don't understand. I can't ask him if he works for our enemy. It's an insult.

**Johnstone** You think I'm daft, don't you. We don't have to *see* him.

**Shahin** *doesn't understand.* **Johnstone** *enjoys the control, brightens.*

**Johnstone** Come on. I'll get this.

*He stands, reaching for money, knocks his tea over, catches the cup, the tea flooding down his front.*

**Johnstone**  Aw. . .

**Shahin** *puts a hand to her face, starts to laugh.* **Johnstone** *looks at her, inert, dripping.*

**Woman** (*O.O.S.*)  Bravo.

*The Greeks sit smiling at the scene. The husband mimes applause.*

*Interior: First Floor Apartment Corridor – Day*

**Shahin** and **Johnstone** *move towards us down the carpeted corridor,* **Johnstone** *in the lead. He walks quickly, eyes on flat numbers.*

**Johnstone** (*on the move*)  You need some info on a piece of real estate, ask the builders. They'll know who's moving in. Probably tell us what they're having for breakfast.

*They stop by a door at the end of the corridor* **Johnstone** *hesitates.*

**Johnstone**  You wanna knock first? (**Shahin** *gives him a weary look.*) Alright, alright. (*He makes a show of sizing up the door, decides to knock – it swings open.*) Hey, it's open.

**Johnstone** *stands back to let* **Shahin** *enter, glances uncertainly along the corridor, follows.*

*Interior: First Floor Apartment, Living Room – Day*

*Shot of a trestle table, a carpet layer's knife, shards of underfelt amongst the litter on top.* **Shahin** *enters the frame, take something from the table. We see it is the Storeman's woolly hat.* **Shahin** *looks at it, trying to place it. Over this, we hear* **Johnstone**, *confidence growing, heading for the bedrooms.*

**Johnstone** (*O.O.S.*)  Anyone home?

**Shahin** *looks across the room. From her P.O.V., we see a rolled up Persian carpet, propped against the wall.*

**Johnstone** *suddenly appears, rushing from the bedroom, ashen faced.*

**Johnstone** (*a whisper*)  There's a bloke in there. A priest. They're – (*a gesture*) It's the fucking Ayatollah.

**Shahin** *sees he means it, picks up her bag.*

**Shahin**  Okay. Let's go.

*As they make for the front door,* **Bamdaad**, *can of coke and plastic cup in hand, comes through it, steps into the room. He looks at* **Shahin** *and* **Johnstone**, *puzzled.*

**Bamdaad** (*slow*)  Salam.

**Johnstone**  What's going on?

**Bamdaad** (*curt*)  This apartment is sold. There is nothing for you here. (*He gestures to the door.*) Please.

**Johnstone**  Wait a minute. It was on the list. You gonna pay her?

**Bamdaad**  A mistake. (*To* **Shahin**.) Estebah showdeh. (*To* **Johnstone**.) Please. Another time.

*He pulls the ring on the coke can, prepares to pour. The flush is heard in the bathroom.* **Bamdaad** *looks at* **Shahin**. **Johnstone** *turns towards the sound. The* **Mullah**, *adjusting his robes, walks into the room, peers at* **Johnstone**. *Beyond him, the Storeman appears, takes in the scene, retreats.*

**Mullah** (*to* **Bamdaad**, *in Farsi*)  Who is the boy?

**Bamdaad** (*in Farsi*)  A messenger.

**Johnstone**  I didn't know you were. . . (*He gestures to* **Shahin**.) She's Iranian. I'm just passing through.

**Bamdaad** (*to* **Johnstone**)  He speaks no English. (*To* **Mullah**, *in Farsi*.)  They're going. I'm sorry. . .

*The* **Mullah** *silences him with a wave, holds out his hand, eyes on* **Shahin**. **Bamdaad** *pours the coke, hands it to the* **Mullah**. *The* **Mullah** *sips, turns his back on* **Shahin**, *sits.*

**Bamdaad** *goes to the flat door, holds it open.* **Shahin** *hurries towards it, her face taut.* **Bamdaad** *stops her.*

**Bamdaad**  I'm in business, Miss Mohamedi. If we want a little piece of home, we must have a little piece of Khomeini.

**Shahin** *pushes past, goes down the corridor.* **Johnstone** *watches, turns to* **Bamdaad**.

**Johnstone**  She thinks you've been talking.

**Bamdaad** (*cool*)  I find her husband. I give her work. What more does she want?

*The* **Mullah** *calls from the living room.*

**Bamdaad**   Perhaps if she cover her face there would be nothing to talk about.

**Johnstone** *nods, thoughtful.*

*Interior:* **Shahin**'s *Flat, Entrance Hall – Day*

*Shot of the door, a hall table on the right. We hear* **Shahin** *and* **Johnstone**, *voices raised as they come up the path. The door flies open.* **Shahin** *steps in first, dumps her bag.* **Johnstone** *follows, closing the door.*

**Shahin**   Don't you see. Hezbollahs are government. This priest –

**Johnstone**   Not over there they aren't.

*He flicks through a pile of letters on the hall table.* **Shahin** *sits on the stairs, head in hands.*

**Shahin**   What if he tells him what we have done.

**Johnstone** *turns, leans against the table.*

**Johnstone** (*sighs*)   If Bamdaad's selling to the guys who are trying to get you deported, he's not gonna tell them he's fixed things so you can stay. Use your head.

*A door opens down the hall.* **Kalinowski** *comes out, a letter in his hand.*

**Kalinowski**   I think this is your lucky day. (*He winks at* **Shahin** – *gives her the letter.*) I signed for it.

*He goes off, chuckling.* **Shahin** *tears open the letter, reads,* **Johnstone** *waits.*

**Shahin**   From Home Office. They want to see us. (*She looks up.*) In Dover.

*Interior: Train, London to Dover – Day*

**Shahin** *and* **Johnstone** *face each other at a corner table of the buffet car. The buffet is closed, the car largely empty.* **Johnstone** *sits, head bent, hands cupped round a can of Carlsberg. He wears his military shirt and fatigues under his coat. Opposite,* **Shahin** *watches him, waiting for an answer. A photo album, unopened, lies on the table* *between them.*

**Johnstone** (*finally*) Sucra.

**Shahin**  No.

**Johnstone** (*sitting back*)  I give up.

**Shahin**  Soghia. You must try and remember. (*She pushes the album across the table.*) Go through it once more.

**Johnstone**  Look. I've never met your mother. Why pretend? She's in Iran for fuck's sake. (**Shahin** *glowers at him.*) We met at a disco. We decided to get married.

*He drains the last of the can, crushes it.*

**Johnstone**  I'm English. You're my wife. That's it.

**Shahin** *puts the album in her bag, takes out a tie.*

**Shahin** (*offering it*)  Will you put this on?

**Johnstone** (*glancing at it*)  You gotta be joking.

**Shahin** *puts the tie on the table, settles back in her seat, gazes out of the window.* **Johnstone** *looks at her, looks at the tie.*

*Exterior: Dover Harbour – Day*

**Shahin** *and* **Johnstone** *walk towards the immigration offices. A transport policeman stands by the entrance.* **Shahin** *puts her arm through* **Johnstone**'s. *They go inside. A ferry blasts its horn, preparing for departure.*

*Interior: Immigration Offices, Interview Room – Day*

*The room is small, bare, neon-lit, the solitary window offering nothing but a restricted view of a grubby yard. Along one wall, official posters urge vigilance against the enemy beyond the borders: rabid dogs, terrorist bombs, heroin, over-loaded trucks.* **Shahin** *and* **Johnstone** *sit in bucket chairs in front of an empty desk.* **Johnstone** *has removed his coat, put on the tie. They wait.*

**Green**, *balding, in his thirties, leather jacket over spotless shirt, comes through the door behind them, a file in his hand. He goes to the desk.*

**Green** (*on the move*)  Mr and Mrs Johnstone. Sorry to drag you down here. London likes to keep us busy when the ferries are quiet.

*He smiles, drops the file on the desk, returns to the door.*

**Green** If I could just ask you to wait outside Mrs Johnstone. (*He holds the door open.*) There's a coffee machine in the corridor. Twos, fives and tens. Any trouble, give it a thump.

**Shahin** *stands, uncertain of the routine.* **Johnstone**, *nervous, makes to move.*

**Green** Not you, sir. You stay where you are.

**Shahin** *fumbles the photo album from her bag, hands it to* **Johnstone**.

**Shahin** James. Will you take these?

**Johnstone** (*taking it*) Oh. Yeah.

**Green** (*watching*) Get good weather?

**Shahin** *looks at him blankly, en route for the door.*

**Johnstone** We haven't been away yet.

**Green** Ah. (*To* **Shahin**, *as she leaves.*) Won't be long.

*He closes the door, studies* **Johnstone**'s *back.*

*Interior: Immigration Offices, Waiting Room – Day*

*The young Turk, a kit-bag at his feet, sits in the corner of the room, in woolly hat, navy sweater, Sealink logo on the front.* **Shahin** *watches as he smokes, stares at the floor, her hands idly tearing a plastic cup.*

**Johnstone** *appears,* **Shahin** *stands.*

**Johnstone** (*winks*) Right you are Mrs Johnstone.

**Shahin** *looks for reassurance.* **Johnstone** *eyes the Turk, moves past* **Shahin**, *sits.* **Shahin** *goes.*

**Johnstone** (*casual*) Nice day for a sail.

*Interior: Immigration Offices, Interview Room – Day*

**Shahin** *sits facing* **Green**, *the photo album, unopened, on the desk between them.* **Green**, *his jacket off, tie loosened, writes in the file.*

**Green** (*writing*) Nice wedding snaps. We get to see a lot of those. (*He reads what he's written, continues writing.*) When did you decide to marry, Mrs Johnstone?

**Shahin** (*calm*) Three, four months ago. It was raining.

**Green** *puts his pen down, sits back, decides to smile.*

**Green** You were still at college?

**Shahin** No, I'd finished.

**Green** *frowns, bends over the file.*

**Green** You'd applied for a student visa. We saw you in January. What – three, four months ago?

*He lifts the photo album, sits back, flicks through.*

**Shahin** (*unphased*) But you know this. I couldn't pay my fees. (*She smiles.*) James wanted to wait until I was able to complete my course. For me, this was not important. I think it is a woman's job to be with her husband. To make a home. A family.

**Green** *nods slowly, studying the album. He shows* **Shahin** *a print:* **Johnstone** *with the whisky bottle.*

**Green** Can you tell me where this was taken?

**Shahin** *hesitates.* **Green** *watches.*

**Green** Is this your flat?

**Shahin** No. James is a photographer. This was a place he took some pictures.

**Green** He didn't take this.

**Shahin** No. I did.

**Green** It's very good.

**Shahin** We have a lot in common.

**Green** *closes the album, hands it to* **Shahin**. *She goes to put it in her bag.*

**Green** We've received a letter alleging you married Mr Johnstone in order to obtain a visa.

**Shahin** *looks at him, slips the album into her bag.*

**Shahin** I don't understand.

**Green** Before we can accept your application, we have to be satisfied this is not the case.

**Shahin**  Who sent this letter?

**Green**  That I can't say. If the allegation is false — well, these things are best forgotten. (*He closes the file.*) I'm afraid it means you'll have to postpone your trip to Spain a few more weeks.

**Shahin**  I'm not in any hurry, Mr Green.

*Exterior: Seafront, Dover — Day*

**Shahin** *and* **Johnstone** *walk briskly away from the harbour.* **Johnstone** *is laughing, the tension released.*

**Johnstone**  We did it, we did it. I told you it'd be alright. God he was a bastard. D'you know what he asked me? I couldn't believe it. He said — what was it — yeah . . . (*Imitating.*) 'Are you and your wife planning a family?' I thought he was talking about social security or something. Fucking cheek. I nearly hit him. (*He stops, turns to* **Shahin**.) He didn't ask you did he? You know. (**Shahin**, *confused, shakes her head.*) We oughta talk about it. I mean. Just in case.

**Shahin**  Someone sent a letter.

**Johnstone**  Yeah. Probably Kalinowski. Touchy lot, Poles.

**Shahin**  Why? Why would they do this?

**Johnstone** *thinks a moment, shrugs.*

**Johnstone**  Forget it. (*He puts his hands on her shoulders.*) I'm proud of you. It's not easy to deal with those bastards. Stick with me, see, you're laughing.

*He kisses her on the cheek.* **Shahin** *flinches, stares at him.*

**Johnstone**  Never know who's watching.

**Shahin** (*turning*)  Let's go.

**Johnstone**  Where you going?

**Shahin**  The station.

**Johnstone**  We can't go yet. We've gotta celebrate.

*He grins.*

*Interior: Fried Chicken Bar, Dover – Day*

**Johnstone** *has nuggets, chips, coleslaw, two or three different dips all but finished.* **Shahin** *has nothing.* **Johnstone** *offers her coleslaw. She shakes her head.* **Johnstone** *gazes morosely round the bar.*

**Johnstone** You didn't eat first time I met you.

**Shahin** *says nothing.* **Johnstone** *chews.*

**Johnstone** Still. Great to get away.

**Shahin** I want to go home.

**Johnstone** *smashes the table with his fist, the coleslaw rolls off.* **Shahin** *freezes.*

**Johnstone** Look. If it wasn't for me you'd be on the plane by now. Remember that.

**Shahin** *looks down.* **Johnstone** *sees an assistant watching, calms himself. He bends down, picks up the coleslaw, chucks it in his empty chip bag.*

**Johnstone** (*quiet*) I am doing you a very big favour. It's about time I got something in return.

**Shahin** (*ice*) I paid you.

**Johnstone** Not for this. This is a full time job. (*He grabs his coat.*) I'm gonna have a good time. And you're coming with me.

*Interior: Public Bar, Dover – Day*

**Shahin** *sits in the corner of the empty bar, a glass of orange juice in her hand. Two other open bottles of Britvic sit on the table.* **Johnstone** *stands at the bar,* **Shahin**'*s purse in his hand. The barman, one eye on the TV set fixed high on the wall, finishes pouring a pint, puts it on the counter.* **Johnstone** *pays, takes another Britvic, goes to* **Shahin**. *He tosses the purse on the seat.*

**Johnstone** It's empty. You're gonna have to get your Polaroid out. Do some 'page threes'. (**Shahin** *ignores him. He puts the bottle on the table.*) Drink for fuck's sake.

*He returns to the bar, lifts his pint, drinks. The barman talks to the TV set.*

*Exterior: Seafront, Dover – Night*

**Johnstone**, *well sozzled, ambles along a narrow road, heading for Dover Marine.* **Shahin**, *head bowed, keeps her distance, uncertain of his mood.*

**Johnstone**  You know you're very beautiful. Used to be a woman on telly just like you. Turkish Delight. She had . . . eyes.

*He stops, looks across to the beach.* **Shahin** *moves alongside.* **Johnstone** *suddenly grabs her arm, pulls her after him.*

**Johnstone**  Come on, misery guts. Let's leave the country.

*He drags her towards the pebbles, breaks free, disappears down the beach.*

**Shahin** *stands by the sea wall, gazing at the blackness of the channel. From her P.O.V. we see, in the distance, a bonfire on the beach, a few people visible, huddled round the flames.* **Shahin** *shivers. From below the wall, footsteps on the pebbles.* **Johnstone** *pisses fulsomely against the wall. His voice, slurred, remote, floats up from the darkness.*

**Johnstone** (*O.O.S.*)  . . . I love my wife. I do. I love her. She just doesn't understand me. I think . . . I think she's got another man. Yeah. I'm away a lot. Fighting. On the beaches. I don't mind. Really I don't. It's just not fair on the kids. Certainly Mr Arafat. . .

*Silence.* **Shahin** *looks down over the wall.*

*A stone is lobbed, hits the edge of the water with a smack.* **Shahin** *shivers, goes to the top of the steps leading to the beach.*

**Shahin**  James. . . ?

*Nothing.* **Shahin** *slips down the steps, looks along the beach to her left.* **Johnstone** *suddenly grabs her from behind, hugs her.*

**Shahin**  No, James. Stop it.

*They stumble.* **Johnstone** *turns her round, pushes her against the wall, pressing into her.*

**Johnstone**  You're so warm.

**Shahin** *tries to struggle free, hands pushing against his chest.* **Johnstone** *tightens his grip, head buried in her neck.*

**Shahin** James. Please. Listen. Something bad is happening. In Iran. I feel it. My family. Don't. Please. I'm frightened. Help me James. Help me.

**Johnstone** *pulls her head into his, kisses her cheek.*

**Johnstone** I don't want to hurt you. It's alright.

*He slips his hand inside her coat.* **Shahin** *trembles, starts to cry.*

**Shahin** I can't. I can't. Oh James. . .

**Johnstone** *thumps her against the wall, suddenly fierce.*

**Johnstone** Don't *say* that. Look at me. Look at me.

**Shahin** *looks at him, shaking, her eyes wet.* **Johnstone** *wipes the tears from her face with his fingers.*

**Johnstone** You can. Say it.

**Shahin** Please let me. . .

**Johnstone** Say it. Promise. Once, that's all. Promise.

**Shahin** (*finally*) I promise.

**Johnstone** *relaxes his grip.* **Shahin**'s *bag drops onto the pebbles.* **Johnstone** *rubs his face, goes.* **Shahin** *waits, back against the wall.*


*Interior: Train – Night*

*An Englishman, in his fifties, tweed coat, hands in his lap, sits gazing out front, head gently rocked by the motion of the train. A faint smile plays across his face.*

*Reverse shot reveals* **Johnstone** *asleep on* **Shahin**'s *shoulder, her hand held tightly in his.* **Shahin** *looks uncomfortable, aware of the Englishman's gaze. She looks out the window, leans against the head rest, closes her eyes.*


*Exterior: (Dream) – Day*

**Shahin** *labours towards the summit of the hill, her feet bare, her clothes dirty, dishevelled. She has her camera round her neck, the British passport in her hand. On the summit, the* **Man**, *in military uniform, a gun butted against his hip. As* **Shahin** *approaches, we see he is singing, but there is no sound. Instead, we hear a flapping noise.* **Shahin** *reaches the summit, looks out across a dusty plain. Black flags*

166 Leave to Remain

*mark rows of graves, each with a framed picture above it, the frames
bordered with flowers, family mementoes. At one of the graves, the two
women in chadors, one with a frame in her lap. We see the frames are
empty. Suddenly, we hear a burst of machine gun fire.* **Shahin**
*screams.*

*Cut to:*

*Interior:* **Shahin**'*s Bedroom – Night*

**Shahin**, *hands on* **Johnstone**'*s naked back, rears up in pain as*
**Johnstone** *enters her. She cries out.*

**Johnstone** Jamshid. . .

**Johnstone** *grunts, climaxes at once.* **Shahin** *falls back, drained,
exhausted. The magazines slip from the bedside table, splatter slowly to
the floor.*


*Interior:* **Shahin**'*s Bedroom – Day*

*Shot of* **Shahin**'*s empty bed, morning light spilled across it from the
window. The covers are pulled back, the sheets rumpled. In the centre
of the bottom sheet, a small blood stain. To one side, a solitary sock.*

**Shahin**, *fully dressed dips into the frame, hands reaching to strip the
bed. A cupboard door bangs in the kitchen.* **Johnstone** *calls.*

**Johnstone** (*O.O.S.*) In here.

**Shahin** *straightens up, waits. Another door bangs. She goes.*


*Interior:* **Shahin**'*s Flat, Kitchen – Day*

**Johnstone**, *naked but for jeans, searches through the kitchen
cupboards, banging doors as he goes. He's tense, edgy.* **Shahin**
*appears, waits by the table.*

**Johnstone** We need coffee. Bread. (*He finds a jar of olives,
throws it back in disgust.*) And get some potatoes. I'm sick of rice.
It's coming out my ears. (*He crosses to the fridge, looks inside.*)
Milk. There's no milk.

**Shahin** (*quiet*) I'll have to borrow some.

**Johnstone** *slams the fridge door, crosses to her.*

**Johnstone** You don't listen do you? Work. Bamdaad owes you.

I don't care if you have to wear bucket over your head. We need the money.

*He's right in front of her.* **Shahin** *suddenly hits him hard across the face.* **Johnstone** *takes it, returns her stare.* **Shahin** *hits him again, a flurry of slaps.* **Johnstone** *grabs her wrist, forces himself to keep calm.*

**Johnstone** (*slow deliberate*) We're married. It's what married people do.

**Shahin** (*in Farsi*) You stupid boy. . .

**Johnstone** (*pulling on her wrist*) Don't start that. You got something to say, say it. Keep the funny talk for the Home Office.

*He lets her go.* **Shahin** *turns, hurries through to the bedroom, gets her camera bag and coat.* **Johnstone** *keeps his distance, watches from the kitchen doorway.*

**Johnstone** (*finally*) I'll do the shopping. I've a coupla quid.

**Shahin** *ignores him, leaves the bedroom, goes to lock the door.* **Johnstone** *moves across.*

**Johnstone**  Leave it. (**Shahin** *pauses, hand on key.*) Me clothes. I'll get arrested if I go out like this.

*He runs a hand across his chest.* **Shahin** *gives him the key.* **Johnstone** *puts his hand on her shoulder.*

**Johnstone** (*quiet*) It doesn't have to be this way. It could be nice. We could go places. Do things.

**Shahin** *pushes past him, goes.* **Johnstone** *watches her leave. He broods a moment, gives the door a sudden, vicious kick.*

*Interior: Mansion Block, Stairway — Day*

**Shahin** *moves towards us along the carpeted corridor, camera bag on her shoulder, making for the stairs. She slows, stops. From her P.O.V., we see two women in chadors moving up the stairs. The second woman has a picture frame under her arm. She glances at* **Shahin.**

**Man** (*O.O.S.*)  Miss Mohamedi?

**Shahin** *whips round, startled. The* **Iranian Man** *stands behind her. He smiles.*

**Man**  Mr Bamdaad told me you were here. (*He reaches inside his* *jacket, produces an envelope.*) We've been trying to reach you.

*He offers* **Shahin** *the envelope.* **Shahin** *looks at it, the official Embassy motif in the corner.*

**Man**  It's about your money. From your father.

**Shahin** *takes the envelope.*

**Man**  It went to the wrong address. We didn't know you'd moved.

*The* **Man** *goes down the corridor.*

*Interior: Second Floor, Iranian Embassy – Day*

*The room is large, bare, uncarpeted.* **Shahin** *sits on a wooden bench in headscarf and glasses. In front of her, a bearded* **Embassy Official** *sits in an armchair. At his side, a small coffee table with a folder on it. Above the table, a picture of Khomeini and several slogans, in Farsi and English (NOT EAST, NOT WEST: ISLAMIC REPUBLIC OF IRAN; DEATH TO THE SADDAM THE HYPOCRITE; ETC).*

*In the middle of the room, a man kneels praying. He wears a vest and cotton pyjamas. His clothes are neatly piled on the floor behind him.*

*The* **Official** *holds up a picture from a pile on his lap. We recognize* **Javad** *at a demonstration.*

**Official**  Him?

**Shahin**  No.

*The* **Official** *holds up another picture (***Akbar***).* **Shahin** *shakes her head.*

**Shahin**  Why did you send for me?

*The* **Official** *fishes out another picture. He shows it to her: it's* **Jamshid**. **Shahin**'s *hand moves towards her face. The* **Official** *smiles, waits.*

**Shahin**  He was at college here.

**Official**  Did you live together?

**Shahin**  (*shakes her head*) He went back.

*The door opens behind her. Another man enters, prepares to join the first man in prayer.*

**Official**  And you? You're not at college?

**Shahin**  I'm married.

**Official**  Ah yes. How was Dover?

*He puts* **Jamshid**'s *picture, face down on the table.*

**Shahin**  Has anything happened?

*The* **Official** *reflects a moment, gathers up the files.*

**Official**  You must be very careful, sister. We know you have connections with these people. (*He sits back.*) He was trying to leave. The communists always run. They know we will not let them poison our republic. Perhaps there are some things of his you can give us. Papers, books, cassettes. If you help us, there will be no more trouble with your money. You can finish your studies and return to Iran. You must be anxious to see your parents. . .

*He stands, glides out.* **Shahin** *looks at the men praying.*


*Exterior/Interior: Iranian Embassy – Day*

**Shahin** *hurries down the steps of the Embassy, goes to the phone box on the corner. Inside, she takes off her scarf and glasses, loosens her hair. She takes out a 10p, starts to dial, thinks, puts down the phone. She goes.*


*Interior:* **Shahin**'s *Flat, Stairs – Day*

*Shot down the empty stairs. On the edge of the frame,* **Johnstone** *leans against the wall, his lower half in shot.*

*The front door bangs.* **Shahin** *appears, moving towards us up the stairs. She reaches the top of the landing.*

**Johnstone**  We've had a visit.

**Shahin** *looks up.* **Johnstone** *stands by the flat door, cigarette cupped in his hand. He looks shaken.*

**Johnstone**  Two of them. The Polish guy let them in. Must have been watching the house.

**Shahin** *searches his face, sensing he's lying.* **Johnstone** *looks down.*

**Johnstone**  There's a bit of a mess.

**Shahin** *moves quickly into the flat.* **Johnstone** *pulls on his cigarette.*

*Interior:* **Shahin**'s *Flat, Bedroom — Day*

*Shot of the bedroom. The room has been searched. The curtain is pulled back from* **Shahin**'s *worktable, the drawers open, the contents spilled across the floor. The bundle of letters lies strewn across the bed.*

**Shahin** *takes in the scene.* **Johnstone** *moves in behind her.*

**Shahin**  What have you done?

**Johnstone** *goes towards the worktable.*

**Johnstone**  I'll give you a hand.

**Shahin** (*sharp*) Leave it.

**Johnstone**  I was trying to help. What should I have done?

**Shahin**  Just go.

**Johnstone** *retreats, sits on the bed.* **Shahin** *stoops down, starts to gather the photographs from the floor.* **Johnstone** *takes a photo from his pocket, unfolds it, holds it in front of* **Shahin.**

**Johnstone**  Who is this?

**Shahin** *looks at it, goes to take it.* **Johnstone** *holds it out of reach.* **Shahin** *resumes clearing.*

**Shahin** (*quiet*) Someone. . .

**Johnstone**  What?

**Shahin**  Someone I know. It's nothing.

**Johnstone**  What d'you mean nothing. (*He nods to the recess.*) There's a whole wall of them in there.

**Shahin** *stands, a sheaf of pictures in her hand. The argument flares rapidly.*

**Shahin**  These are my things you have. . .

**Johnstone**  Just answer the question. . .

**Shahin**  . . . no *right* to be in here, we agreed. . .

**Johnstone**  . . . tell me who it is. . .

**Shahin**  . . . you don't, you don't. . .

*Silence.* **Johnstone** *waits.* **Shahin** *looks at him.*

**Shahin** (*moving*) I can't explain. . .

**Johnstone** (*grabbing her arm*) Who is it?

**Shahin** (*fast, fierce*) It's my fiancé.

**Johnstone** *hits her across the face.* **Shahin** *catches her breath. They look at each other.*

**Johnstone** Jesus. (*Taking it in.*) You trying to make me – your fiancé? I'm stuck in here all day in this – pantomime and you're out there with your fiancé?

**Shahin** You don't understand. He's not here. . .

**Johnstone** I know everything about your family. Everything. Not a word. Not a mention. Give me those.

*He tries to grab the pictures in* **Shahin**'s *hand. They struggle.*

**Shahin** (*in Farsi*) No, no. He's gone. He's gone. They've taken him. . .

**Johnstone** I'll kill the bastard. He lays a finger on you. . .

**Johnstone** *gets the pictures, tears them up, throws the pieces at* **Shahin**. **Shahin** *sinks to her knees, starts to cry.*

**Shahin** You don't understand. He went back. He wanted to go. (*She shakes her head, wretched.*) I couldn't. I couldn't. I was too frightened.

**Johnstone** *watches her, hurt, confused. He rubs his face, fighting for control.*

**Johnstone** You think I got into this 'cos I didn't have anything better to do? Is that it? 'I'll just go get hitched before the shops close.' This has cost me. I could be half way across Europe by now. Off with that Aussie slag. Anyone.

**Shahin** Then why don't you go?

**Johnstone** What? Don't give me that. You wouldn't last a week. You really think you can pull if off, don't you. Stay here, tart yourself up, land some cushy job. It's finished. There are no jobs. Use your eyes for Christ's sake. Everyone's leaving. All the smart people fucked off years ago. (*He turns away, paces.*) I don't believe this. Every time. Every fucking time.

**Shahin** *tries to get to her feet.* **Johnstone** *catches her, pushes her to the floor.*

**Johnstone**  You stay there. I haven't finished yet.

**Shahin** *waits.* **Johnstone** *snatches a pile of letters from the bed, holds them out.*

**Johnstone**  These his? (**Shahin** *nods.*) Come on then. Let's hear it. Read one. Come on. (*He stuffs a letter in her hand.*) I gotta get to know this guy. He sounds like he's pretty special.

**Shahin** (*looking at the letter*)  It's nothing –

**Johnstone**  Read it. I wanna know. From the beginning.

**Shahin** *opens the letter, translates, her voice faltering, frightened by* **Johnstone**'s *violence.*

**Shahin**  'My dear professor.' It's a – I don't know English word. She makes, he makes joke. Because I study so much. (*She wipes her eyes, clears her throat.*) 'The plane was late, so –' (*She stops, looks at* **Johnstone**.) Please. Don't make me –

**Johnstone** *drops to his knees, grabs her head.*

**Johnstone**  Read it.

**Shahin**  'The plane was late, so I two more hour in England. Two hour to think me, to think why I leaving. I know I can't –'

*She tries to twist free of* **Johnstone**'s *grip.*

**Shahin**  This word, I –

**Johnstone**  Read it.

**Shahin** *closes her eyes, recites the letter from memory, each phrase a physical effort.*

**Shahin**  'I can't live in exile . . . I dream of Iran . . . How one day . . . we will walk together . . . and laugh to think . . . we were not free . . .'

**Johnstone**  You're making it up. That isn't here.

*He snatches the letter, gets up, looks at it, unable to read a word. He turns on* **Shahin**.

**Johnstone**  Fuck it, I *married* you. You're my *wife*.

*A beat. They look at each other across the continents, separate, uncomprehending.* **Johnstone** *wheels round, close to tears, heads for the door.* **Shahin** *sits immobile, gazing at the floor.*

*Interior:* **Shahin**'s *Flat, Living Room – Day*

**Johnstone** *emerges from his bedroom, suitcase in hand, a bundle of clothes under his arm. He dumps the case, throws back the lid, drops the clothes inside.*

**Shahin** *appears at her bedroom door, pale, exhausted, watches as* **Johnstone** *crosses to the bathroom then returns with toilet gear and a handful of dirty washing.*

**Johnstone** (*as he moves*)  No one walks over me. No one. All that stuff about protecting your family. You were covering for him, weren't you? The big hero. Out there. Fighting for freedom. Well, I got plans too. And I'm not hanging round.

*He grabs the case, goes, slams the door.* **Shahin** *pulls the ring off her finger, goes to throw it after* **Johnstone**, *can't find the effort, let's it drop.*

*Interior:* **Shahin**'s *Flat, Bathroom – Night*

**Shahin** *sits in the bath, her hair loose. The bathroom light is not on. She puts a hand on the edge of the bath, slips forward until her hair and face are submerged.*

*Interior:* **Shahin**'s *Flat, Kitchen – Night*

*Close shot of the sink, the taps running, two black and white prints under the water.*

**Shahin** *fishes out the prints, pegs them to a line strung across the kitchen. She is dressed, her hair wrapped in a red towel. She turns off the tap, steps back, looks at the prints. She unwinds the towel, feels her hair. Water from the prints drips onto the floor. We scan the pictures – shots of Iranian prisoners, men and women.*

*Interior:* **Shahin**'s *Flat, Bedroom – Night*

*The enlarger and developing trays are set out on the worktable.* **Shahin** *lowers the enlarger, brings an image into focus, stops down the lens. She snaps on a safelight, slides a piece of photographic paper under the masking frame. She fiddles with the frame, unable to get the* *paper in straight, bangs the frame in frustration. Her hand shakes.*

**Shahin** *starts the timer. From her P.O.V. we see the negative image of* **Jamshid.** *The seconds tick by.* **Shahin***'s hand enters the frame, stops the clock.* **Shahin** *sweeps the clock off the table. A bottle of developer is knocked over. We hold on the image of* **Jamshid. Shahin** *leaves the frame. We hear a door bang.*


*Exterior: Rear of Chicken Bar – Night*

*Shot along the alley, the back entrance to the bar on the right. At the far end, a police patrol car, the passenger door swung open.*

**Shahin** *turns into the alley, makes for the bar. She sees the car, slows, stops. In the yards down from the bar, two* **Asian Dishwashers**, *an* **Italian Waitress** *and a* **Caretaker** *stand in the shadows watching, waiting.*

*Suddenly, the door to one of the delivery bays is pushed up. A* **Policeman,** *flashlight in hand, emerges from the darkness. The* **Caretaker** *looks at* **Shahin,** *turns away, disappears inside the building two doors down. The* **Policeman** *moves off down the alley towards the car.* **Shahin** *hesitates, goes to the back door of the bar.*


*Interior: Chicken Bar, Corridor/Kitchen – Night*

**Shahin** *moves along the empty corridor towards the kitchen. As she passes the toilet door, it opens a fraction.* **Shahin** *turns.* **Raouf** *appears, signals her to avoid the kitchen.* **Shahin** *goes to him.*

**Shahin**  What is it?

**Raouf** *goes to answer, sees someone behind her, closes the door.* **Shahin** *turns.* **Mina** *appears from the kitchen, removing her uniform. She hangs her overall on a peg, goes to take her coat, sees* **Shahin.** *The two women look at each other.* **Mina** *gives a tight smile. An* **Immigration Officer,** *in her forties, plain clothes, appears behind* **Mina,** *reaches for her coat.*

**Officer** (*to* **Mina.**) This yours?

**Mina** *nods, turns back into the kitchen. The* **Officer** *takes the coat, follows her.* **Shahin** *goes after them, turns into the kitchen.*

**Javad** *stands by the fryer dropping chicken pieces into the fat. As* **Shahin** *appears, he looks up, impassive.* **Ben** *serves at the front of the bar, one eye on the activity behind him. Across from* **Javad,** *in the* *centre of the kitchen, a* **Second Immigration Officer** *leans against a table flipping through a notebook. The* **First Officer** *and* **Mina** *wait nearby.* **Henry**, *agitated, works on the* **Second Officer**.

**Henry**  Look mister. She not finish her three hour. She got work to do. These people wanna eat. (*She sees* **Mina** *with her uniform off.*) What you doing? (*To* **Officer**.) This is crazy. What my boss say you kidnap my woman.

**Second Officer**  We'll talk to your boss.

*A* **Third Officer** *comes through the front of the bar, a green registration book in his hand. The* **Second Officer** *gives him a questioning look. The* **Third Officer** *tosses the book on the table.*

**Third Officer**  He's O.K.

*The* **Second Officer** *looks at* **Javad**, *nods.* **Javad** *moves to the freezer, reaches for a fresh tray of chicken bits. The* **Second Officer** *sees* **Shahin**, *turns to* **Henry**.

**Second Officer**  Who's that?

**Henry** (*dismissive*)  Customer.

**Shahin** *moves forward, fixes on the* **Second Officer**.

**Shahin**  Why are you taking her?

**Second Officer** (*ignoring* **Shahin** *– to* **Henry**)  Lost her way, has she?

*He starts to leave, beckons the other* **Officers** *to follow.*

**Second Officer**  Let's go.

**Shahin** (*level*)  I asked you a question.

**Henry** (*a gesture*)  Shahin. . .

*The* **Second Officer** *stops, turns, studies* **Shahin**'s *face.* **Henry** *and* **Javad** *exchange looks,* **Javad** *a tray of chicken bits in his hand.* **Mina** *watches, expressionless.*

**Second Officer**  If I were you miss, I'd leave it there.

**Shahin**  She has travelled two thousand mile. Alone. She has no friends here. Only us. She wants nothing from you. When she is ready, she'll go back. Why you treat her like an animal?

**Second Officer**  Now wait a minute. . .

**Javad** (*over him, in Farsi*) Leave it, Shahin. . .

**Shahin** (*flaring*) You think she too stupid to carry her coat.

*The* **First Officer**, *bemused, looks down at* **Mina**'s *coat.* **Shahin** *flares at the* **Second Officer**, *defiant. He stiffens a little, sizing her up.*

**First Officer** (*low*) Jesus wept.

*A* **Customer** *appears at the side of the bar, hunting for attention.*

**Customer** Any chance of a bit of action round here? The guy up front's run off his feet.

*All eyes turn to the* **Customer**. *He smiles.* **Mina** *seizes her chance, makes a dash for the back door. The* **First Officer** *tries to grab her, misses, collides with* **Javad.** *The tray of chicken pieces goes flying, clatters to the floor. The* **Customer** *gawps.* **Shahin** *darts out after* **Mina** *as the* **First Officer** *pushes* **Javad** *aside.*


*Interior: Chicken Bar, Corridor – Night*

**Shahin** *runs down the corridor,* **Mina** *already out into the alley. Behind her, we hear the* **Second Officer** *shout to the* **Third** *to cover the front entrance.* **Shahin** *bangs the toilet door as she passes.* **Raouf** *steps out, protesting.*

**Raouf** Completely empty in here, sir. Totally clean. . .

*The* **Officers** *collide with* **Raouf**, *push him away.*

**First Officer** (*winded*) What the fuck. . . ?

**Second Officer** Come on, come on. . .

**Raouf** *flattens himself against the wall, terrified.*


*Exterior: Rear of Chicken Bar – Night*

**Shahin** *stands in the centre of the alley watching* **Mina** *run. Behind her, the patrol car starts up,* **Shahin** *caught in the glare of the headlights. The car races towards her, brakes, blares it horn.* **Shahin** *turns, refusing to move. The* **First Officer** *reaches her, pushes her out of the way.*

**First Officer** Get out of it.

**Shahin** *falls. The* **Two Officers** *leap into the patrol car. The car* *speeds away up the alley, stops at the top, starts to take a right, goes left.* **Shahin** *watches.* **Mina** *has disappeared.* **Raouf** *comes out of the bar, quickly crosses to* **Shahin***. Beyond him, the dishwashers and waitress stand watching.*

**Raouf** (*pulling her up*) Easy. You O.K.?

**Shahin** I'm fine.

*She brushes herself down.* **Raouf** *steers her to the door.*

**Shahin** Wait.

*She looks towards the top of the alley. From her P.O.V. we see the patrol car double back, set off in the opposite direction.*

**Raouf** (*O.O.S.*) Henry got her false papers.

**Shahin** (*O.O.S.*) I know. It should have been me.

*We hold on the alley, dark, empty. In the distance, a siren wails.*

*Interior: Chicken Bar – Night*

*The bar is closed, the lights at the front off.* **Shahin, Henry** *and* **Raouf** *sit at a table in the bar, light angled across them from the kitchen.* **Raouf** *smokes,* **Henry** *sips vodka, the bottle on the table,* **Shahin** *toys with a tea.*

*Beyond them, on the edge of the shot,* **Javad** *stands by the payphone, address book open on the top, making a call in Farsi.*

**Henry** (*gloomy*) You were right. Kitchen is bad place.

**Raouf** Hey. It's not your fault. She knew the risk. Tell her, Shahin.

**Shahin** *looks up from her tea, lost in thought. She turns to* **Henry***.*

**Shahin** I've been to Embassy. I was on my way to tell you. Jamshid's been arrested.

**Henry** *blinks, waits for more.* **Shahin** *reaches for the vodka bottle.*

**Shahin** (*nods*) Can I?

**Henry** Here. Let me.

**Henry** *pours a dash of vodka into a cup, gives it to* **Shahin***.* **Raouf** *sits back in his seat.*

**Raouf** This has been a bad day, sister. A bad day.

**Shahin** *dips her finger into the cup, tastes it.*

**Henry** Drink.

**Shahin** *drinks a small mouthful, makes a face. She holds the cup in both hands, swills the liquid, watches it settle.*

**Shahin** When he left I was so angry. I couldn't find the reason. Why fight those old men. They have no laughter, nothing gentle. (*She sips.*) Then the stories started. I didn't know what to believe. Bad things happened in Shah's time, but we had a good life. Jamshid wrote. Simple things. Duty. Freedom. Sometimes, after he went to the mountains, he sent a little flower. I could smell it on the paper. All that way and it was still there. But there was less and less about me. About us. (*She looks at* **Henry**.) I had to do it Henry. I had to try. Otherwise I was just running away.

**Javad** *appears behind* **Raouf**. *He has heard* **Shahin**.

**Javad** Jamshid?

**Shahin** *looks up, nods.*

**Javad** When?

**Shahin** (*getting up*) Not now, Javad. We'll talk later.

**Javad** (*to* **Henry**) Ramin's taking Mina to Manchester. I'll go Saturday.

**Henry** *nods, turns to* **Shahin**.

**Henry** I take you home. I got new cupboards. This big.

*She demonstrates.* **Shahin** *smiles.*

**Shahin** Thank you.

**Javad** *and* **Raouf** *head for the back.* **Henry** *calls after them.*

**Henry** We open tomorrow, ten o'clock. You late, you die. (*She turns to* **Shahin**, *sighs.*) What we doing here?

*Interior: Chicken Bar, Back Corridor — Night.*

**Shahin** *stands in the corridor, waiting for* **Henry**. *The last lights blink off in the bar. We hear a jangle of keys,* **Henry** *singing to herself, high, tuneless. Finally,* **Henry** *appears, keys in hand, pulling on her coat. She stops by* **Shahin**, *looks at her in the gloom.*